Steam Oven Christmas

Beautiful, approachable recipes for the festive season using your Combination Steam Oven

EMILY RHODES

First Edition

Published by MacAllan Press, Australia
©Emily Rhodes 2022
All rights reserved.

No portion of this book may be reproduced or transmitted in any form by any means, electronic, mechanical, photocopying or other, without permission of the author.

For permissions contact: emily@steamandbake.com
Text, photography, design and formatting by Emily Rhodes
Visit Emily's website at www.steamandbake.com

Welcome!

Steam Oven Christmas is about celebratory recipes which bring everyone to the table for delicious holiday eating. This is the food I cook for family and friends, things which are staples of my own festive occasions.

Although you'll find mostly steam and combination steam recipes within these pages, I have included a handful of 'regular' recipes which don't require any steam. This is intentional! Part of the joy of having a combi steam oven is the flexibility to mix steam oven recipes with traditional favorites, creating an exciting and delicious menu using different cooking methods. I hope you'll find that getting great use from your combi steam oven and impressing your guests is an added bonus to the delicious food!

I love getting feedback about what's cooking in my readers' combi steam ovens, and hope to hear that you've discovered a new Christmas favorite in the pages which follow.

Merry Christmas

Emily x

CONTENTS

CHRISTMAS MORNING

Spiced Orange and Cranberry Muffins	18
Caramel Breakfast Scrolls	20
Sous Vide Egg Bites	22
Brunch Tarts	24
Cheese and Spinach French Toast Sandwiches	28
Choc Hazelnut and Strawberry French Toast Sandwiches	30

STARTERS

Roasted Pears with Prosciutto and Blue Cheese	34
Puff Pastry Cheese Straws	36
Three-Cheese Stuffed Mushrooms	38
Olive, Pesto and Cherry Tomato Tartlets	40
Pumpkin Dinner Rolls	42

THE MAIN EVENT

Port and Redcurrant Glazed Ham	46
Christmas Roast Duck	48
Salmon with Maple Butter, Almonds and Dill Sauce	50
Whole Roasted Cauliflower with Moorish Spices	52
Turkey Breast Roll with Apricots and Walnuts	56
Sous Vide Turkey Breast with Herbs and Garlic	58
Classic Roast Turkey	60
Turkey Pot Pies	64
Turkey Salad with Vietnamese Dressing	66
Ham and Cheese Enchiladas	68

SIDES

Crispy Roasted Potatoes	**72**
Steam Oven Mashed Potatoes	**74**
Green Beans with Almonds	**76**
Carrots, Ricotta and Lemon	**78**
Christmas Rice Salad	**80**
Brussels Sprouts and Couscous Salad	**82**
Bacon Wrapped Sausages	**84**
Sour Cherry and Pecan Stuffing	**86**

DESSERT

Crème Caramel	**90**
Chocolate Pots de Creme	**92**
Chocolate and Raspberry Roulade	**94**
Fig, Apricot and Orange Christmas Pudding	**96**
Individual Steamed Christmas Puddings	**98**
Christmas Cheesecake	**102**
Basque Burnt Cheesecake	**104**
Mint Chocolate Cheesecake	**106**

GIFTING

Sweet and Spicy Party Nuts	**110**
Spiced Fruit Mince Pies	**112**
Panforte with Ginger, Apricots and Macadamias	**114**
Traditional Shortbread	**116**
Best Ever Chocolate Gingerbread Cookies	**118**
Burnt Caramel Truffles	**120**

The Steam and Bake story

Steam and Bake started in early 2014, as a tiny little blog where I thought I'd share a few combi steam recipes. I was working for an Australian importer of premium European appliance brands, developing recipes and training, and demonstrating kitchen appliances to consumers.

I had been on a steep learning curve with steam ovens. I loved the technology and the cooking results, but there really wasn't much guidance out there. My colleagues and I were competent cooks, yet every new dish was a case of trial and error. There weren't (still aren't) any good formulas for converting dishes to combi steam, and the only cookbooks available were manufacturer-specific ones with recipes I didn't find appealing. I had noticed a big swing towards people purchasing combi steam ovens, but they all had the same question: 'where can I get help and recipes'?

I was annoyed that I couldn't direct people to a website or book for help. And I figured if every combi steam oven owner I met was asking the question, there must be countless others around the world wondering the same thing.

That was that, really. I got online, learned a lot about blogs and websites, and started posting recipes. In the years since, the popularity of combi steam ovens has exploded and I've been thrilled to connect with tens of thousands of cooks from around the world. I never imagined so many people would find the blog, or that I'd still be doing it today!

I love sharing my recipes and ideas, and I love the shared community that's grown up around Steam and Bake. It's one of fellow food-lovers who want to learn, cook better food and help each other.

If you'd like to be part of the community, come and join us! Become an email subscriber at steamandbake.com (I send my subscribers all the best stuff), and join the Combi Steam Cooking Facebook group to chat with like-minded steam oven owners from around the world.

AN IMPORTANT NOTE ON HUMIDITY (STEAM) LEVELS WHEN USING COMBINATION STEAM SETTINGS

The recipe settings in this book list a humidity level as well as an oven function (steam or combi steam, or occasionally straight convection) and temperature.

Many combi steam ovens have the option of selecting a humidity or steam level when using a combination steam setting. Some use percentages, while others have a low, medium, or high steam distinction.

Some combi steam ovens have no option to alter humidity, offering instead a combi steam or convection steam function where the appliance determines the amount of steam dependent on temperature.

It is impossible to write recipes which cover the variable oven settings across all brands, but it's important to remember that whatever your brand of combi steam oven, the recipes in these pages will work for you with a few minimal tweaks! I have cooked in steam ovens with percentages, with pre-set levels, and without any ability to set humidity levels at all. They all achieve fabulous results.

Here's how to approach things if your oven doesn't offer humidity percentages:

- If you have a combi steam oven with no option to select humidity or steam levels, simply use the combi steam setting and the oven temperature listed. Your oven will work out humidity for you, although you may need to adjust cooking times slightly depending on your oven.

- If your appliance gives the option to select low, medium or high steam levels (instead of percentages) when you cook with combi steam settings, use the following guide to select the right option:
    - **Recipes calling for less than 40% humidity: low steam**
    - **Recipes calling for 40-60% humidity: medium steam**
    - **Recipes calling for more than 60% humidity: high steam**

A NOTE ON COOKING TIMES

Because of the many ways combi steam ovens are manufactured, and their differing methods of providing steam for cooking functions, cooking times are always a guide.

I am confident in all the recipes which follow, but you should be mindful that in some ovens they may take a few minutes less to cook; in others a few minutes more. Once you've been using your oven for a while, you'll find you can predict if dishes may cook faster or slower.

Kitchen Essentials

Apart from my combi steam oven, I would not be without the following items in my kitchen.

Scales
I know scales are not commonplace in American kitchens, but if you love to cook and don't have a set, I urge you to do so! Although I write recipes in both metric and US customary measures, I first and foremost cook by metric (weight). It's much more reliable and you'll get consistent, repeatable results, especially when it comes to baking. Slimline digital scales are inexpensive and don't take up much space in your kitchen.

Stand mixer
A strong pair of hands and a spoon replace most of a mixer's tasks, but if you enjoy baking a good mixer will always be welcome. Mine is a KitchenAid; the first birthday gift my husband ever bought me. It's still going strong many years later and was worth his investment. I use it for doughs and batters, whipping cream and for lots of other tiresome mixing jobs.

Food processor
A food processor or blender is handy for pureeing, whether that's a full food processor or a smaller 'stick' or immersion blender. I frequently use my processor to make pastry and chop or grind fruits and nuts.

Mixing bowls

The bowl I use most frequently is the one from my mixer. I also have an assortment of lightweight stainless steel bowls, a couple of glass ones and a Pyrex measuring jug. Anything large enough to contain your ingredients is just fine, although my preference is to stay away from plastic bowls. They hold smells from strong savory or spicy foods, unleashing them later into your carefully prepared baked goods.

Measuring cups and spoons

One decent set of measuring cups with 1/4, 1/3, 1/2 and 1 cup is really all you need. The same when it comes to spoons; a set with 1/4, 1/2 and 1 teaspoon plus 1 tablespoon sizes is suffice for most people.

Make sure you know whether your cup and spoon measures are US Customary/Imperial or Metric, as they differ slightly. It doesn't matter for many dishes but when it comes to baking, the difference between an American tablespoon (3 teaspoons) or a Metric tablespoon (4 teaspoons) can make a big difference to your results. I discuss measurements more on the Conversions page.

Spatulas, stirrers and whisks

I have two sizes of heatproof flexible silicone spatulas; shaped like shallow spoons with defined edges, they are brilliant for mixing thick batters and scraping out bowls.

I use an olive wood angled spatula for stirring vegetables while sauteeing. It's sturdy and great for getting into the corners of saucepans.

Sometimes a whisk will be called for; I use a medium sized metal balloon whisk.

Baking trays and pans
Most combi steam ovens come with a few stainless steel or enamel baking trays. These have the advantage of fitting perfectly into your oven but are rarely the size you need for baking.

Any oven proof tray or pan can be used in your steam oven. For cake and muffin baking I keep a couple of 9x13 inch (23x33cm) rectangles, a couple of sizes of round cake pans and a muffin pan handy. For bread, one or two loaf pans are useful.

If you are baking pastry or dough in your combi steam oven, try to use dark coloured baking sheets and pans. They offer better browning to the undersides of your baked goods than light coloured metals. I have several dark metal cookie sheets and a few patty pan trays for little tarts and pies.

Cast iron bakeware
I have a number of enameled cast iron pots; the most versatile is a low-sided Le Creuset pan with a domed lid. I use it almost daily for sweet and savory cooking. It presents nicely from oven to table, and the heavy material conducts heat well. I much prefer it to glass bakeware in most cases.

Microplane grater
I bought my first Microplane almost 20 years ago, and it's still going strong. It can't be beaten for ginger, garlic and citrus zest.

Conversions

Because I have a global readership, I allow for both Metric and US Customary units of measurement in all my recipes.

The recipes in this book are written using US Customary/Imperial measurements first and Metric measurements second. I give oven temperatures in both Fahrenheit and Celsius for each recipe.

Please note my recipes use Metric cup and spoon equivalents. There are differences in tablespoon and cup measurements between US Customary and Metric standards:

- 1 Metric tablespoon is 20ml, while US Customary/Imperial is 15ml.
- 1 Metric cup is 250ml, US Customary/Imperial is 240ml.

Readers with US Customary measuring utensils should use 4 teaspoons where a tablespoon is called for, and slightly overfill full cup measures.

Glossary

Butter
I always use unsalted butter for baking, adding salt separately. This gives more control over how salty (or not) a finished dish is.

If I call for 'soft' butter I mean something you can easily cut into cubes, but where the cubes will stay distinct and sharp-edged unless you squash them.

Occasionally a recipe might require 'very soft' butter, which is exactly what it sounds like. You should be able to squash very soft butter easily with the back of a spoon.

Superfine (caster) sugar
Identical in composition to granulated white sugar, but with much finer grains. I use superfine sugar in almost all my baking, it's far quicker to mix and dissolve than granulated sugar. I'm aware it's difficult to find in some parts of the world; if that's the case, granulated sugar is a fine substitute but may require more mixing to dissolve.

Eggs
I use what are called extra large eggs in Australia. They average 60g (just a touch over 2oz). I use free range or pasture-grown eggs for bird welfare reasons.

Flour
Unless otherwise stated, the recipes in this book refer to regular wheat flour. In the USA this is all-purpose flour, in Australia and the UK, plain flour.

For heavier doughs like breads, I sometimes call for bread flour. You can substitute all-purpose in a pinch, but bread flour (sometimes called baker's flour) has a higher protein content and develops a better gluten structure than all-purpose.

Puff Pastry
I almost never make my own puff pastry. It's tricky and takes a long time. In Australia, pre-made and pre-rolled puff pastry comes packaged in square sheets measuring 30cm/12 inches. If you can't buy pre-rolled, look for a block of puff pastry at the supermarket or ask your local bakery.

Vanilla Extract and Beans
I use vanilla a lot in baking. I always go for pure vanilla extract rather than synthetic vanilla essence. It's far more expensive but worth the splurge. The taste and aroma of real vanilla cannot be recreated by any synthetic product.

In some recipes I call for a vanilla bean with the seeds scraped out. Look for beans which are plump and soft; if they're dry and snap when you bend them, they're old and better used to scent a bag of sugar than for cooking.

Salt
Unless otherwise stated, I use fine-grained salt for baking. Where flaky salt is called for, I use Maldon salt flakes.

Christmas Morning

Christmas breakfast should be special, but it also needs to be relaxed.

I want something we can serve and eat with minimal effort between opening gifts, cooking for a big lunch and playing with whatever Santa brings.

The following dishes fit the bill nicely. You might have to do some preparation the night before, but they come to the table without fuss on the day. None need more than a side plate and fork for serving.

Spiced Orange and Cranberry Muffins

Caramel Breakfast Scrolls

Sous Vide Egg Bites

Brunch Tarts

Cheese and Spinach French Toast Sandwiches

Choc Hazelnut and Strawberry French Toast Sandwiches

Spiced Orange and Cranberry Muffins

MAKES
12

PREP TIME
10 min

COOKING TIME
12 min

OVEN SETTINGS
350°F/180°C
Combination Steam
30% Humidity

INGREDIENTS

1 3/4 cups (250g) all-purpose (plain) flour
2 1/2 tsp baking powder
1/2 tsp baking soda (bicarbonate soda)
1/2 cup (100g) superfine (caster) sugar
1 tsp ground cinnamon
1 tsp ground ginger
1/4 tsp ground cloves
Zest and juice of 1 orange
1/2 cup (125ml) buttermilk
1/3 cup (75ml) vegetable oil
1 egg
1 cup (120g) dried cranberries
2 Tbsp turbinado sugar

METHOD

1. Preheat your oven to 350°F/180°C, Combination Steam, 30% humidity. Lightly grease a 12 cup standard sized muffin pan and set aside.
2. Put all the dry ingredients into a bowl and stir to combine.
3. Put the orange zest and juice, buttermilk, oil and egg into another bowl and whisk to break up the egg. Pour this wet mix into the dry ingredients and stir gently until it's halfway mixed, with clumps of flour still visible. Add the cranberries and stir until everything is just mixed together. A little lumpy is ok for muffins - if you overmix them the finished texture will be tough.
4. Divide the mixture between the muffin cups and sprinkle with turbinado sugar. Bake until the muffins are just cooked through and golden brown, about 12 minutes. Serve warm. Leftovers can be reheated or toasted and served with butter.

The spicy, fruity aroma of these muffins as they bake makes me think of all the best things about Christmas food. They're comforting without being heavy or too large, which makes them just right if you need something small to tide you over before a huge main event lunch.

Mix up the dry ingredients the night before, if you like, to make the muffins come together faster in the morning.

The turbinado sugar sprinkled on top is optional, though it does lend a really nice crunchy contrast.

Caramel Breakfast Scrolls

MAKES
12
generous scrolls

PREP TIME
40 minutes plus
1hr 10 mins proofing time

COOKING TIME
25 min

OVEN SETTINGS
100°F/38°C
Steam/Dough Proving
Then 350°F/180°C
Combination Steam
30% Humidity

INGREDIENTS

For the dough:

3/4 cup (185ml) whole milk, slightly warmed
1 Tbsp superfine (caster) sugar
2 tsp active dry or instant yeast (see note)
3 eggs, room temperature
6 Tbsp (90g) unsalted butter, very soft
4 cups (485g) all-purpose (plain) flour
1 tsp fine salt

For the caramel:

1/2 cup (125g) unsalted butter
1 cup, firmly packed (200g) brown sugar
1 cup (250ml) pouring cream
1/4 tsp fine salt

For the filling:

1/4 cup, firmly packed (50g) brown sugar
1 tsp ground ginger
1 tsp ground cinnamon
1/2 tsp ground nutmeg
1/4 tsp ground cloves
3 Tbsp (45g) unsalted butter, very soft
2 cups (200g) pecan nuts, finely chopped

METHOD

1. Make the dough. Mix the milk and sugar together in a small bowl, then sprinkle the yeast over the top and leave to sit until it begins to bubble on top, around five minutes.
2. Put the eggs, butter, flour and salt into the bowl of a stand mixer fitted with the dough hook attachment. Give the yeast mixture a stir and tip into the bowl. Mix on low speed for two minutes to combine, then increase speed to medium and mix until smooth

These scrolls are unapologetically sticky, sweet and glorious. At any other time of year it would make more sense to serve them up for a substantial morning tea. If, however, you view Christmas morning as a time of sheer breakfast indulgence, they are worth the effort.

My preferred way of making these is to do the hard work the day before. I make them right up to the end of step seven, then put the dish in the fridge to do the final proof overnight. All you have to do in the morning is remove them from the fridge, turn the oven on and bake. I've outlined a second oven proof below should you wish to make the recipe all in one day.

You'll need a wide, shallow dish for baking. I use a round 12 inch (30cm) low cast iron pan, but a ceramic baking dish will work too. Use a 9x12 inch (23x33cm) rectangular dish if you don't have a round.

A note on yeast: I use active dried yeast. If you're using instant, skip the first step and just mix the yeast, milk and sugar straight in with the dough. It might take a little longer to complete the first proof if you use instant, anywhere up to 60 minutes.

METHOD Continued...

3. Do the first proof. Set oven to dough proofing setting (or steam setting, if you don't have dough proofing), 100°F/38°C. Put the uncovered bowl into the oven for 40 minutes. The dough should have doubled in size; if it hasn't, give it another 15 minutes and check again.

4. While the dough proofs, make the caramel. Put all the ingredients into a medium saucepan and bring to the boil, stirring to combine as the butter melts. Simmer until the caramel has thickened and is a deep golden brown, about 4-5 minutes. Remove from heat and pour into your baking dish, then set aside until cool.

5. Assemble the filling. Mix all the filling ingredients except the nuts together in a small bowl. Set aside.

6. Assemble the scrolls. When the dough has finished the first proof, scrape it out of the bowl onto a floured bench. Gently press to knock out any large air bubbles, then roll it into a rectangle about 16 inches (40cm) wide and 12 inches (30cm) long. Using your fingers, very gently spread the filling over the dough, squashing it out so there's a thin, even layer.

7. Sprinkle half the pecans over the now-cold caramel, and the other half over the sheet of dough. Roll the dough up tightly from the long side, so you have a 16 inch (40cm) long log. Put the entire log into the freezer for 20 minutes to make it easier to cut.

8. Carefully cut the chilled dough into 12 even pieces with a serrated knife. Arrange evenly over the caramel and pecans in the baking dish.

9. Proof the scrolls. If you want to hold off baking, cover with a plastic bag or cling wrap and pop them in the fridge for up to 12 hours. They'll slowly proof and the flavor and texture will be fantastic. If you're baking the same day, set your oven to dough proofing setting (or steam) again, 100°F/38°C. Put the uncovered dish in the oven for 30 minutes. The scrolls should look puffy and be starting to fill out the baking dish.

10. Bake the scrolls: if you've proofed your scrolls in the oven, you can leave them in there while it heats up. If you did the fridge proofing method, remove the dish about an hour before you'd like to bake so they can come up to room temperature. Set oven to 350°F/180°C, Combination Steam, 30% humidity. Bake the scrolls until deep golden brown and risen, about 25 minutes. Leave in the baking dish for 5 minutes before carefully inverting onto a serving platter. Serve warm.

Sous Vide Egg Bites

MAKES
6

PREP TIME
10 min

COOKING TIME
45 min

OVEN SETTINGS
175°F/80°C
Steam
100% Humidity

INGREDIENTS

3 slices streaky bacon, cooked and cut in half

6 eggs

2/3 cup lightly packed (55g) gruyere or other Swiss-style cheese, grated

3 Tbsp (55g) cream cheese; use cottage cheese or cream as substitutes

METHOD

1. Preheat your oven to 175°F/80°C, Steam, 100% humidity. Put your jars into a shallow pan so they're easy to move around.
2. Put one piece of bacon into each jar, pushing it down to the bottom.
3. Put the rest of the ingredients into a blender or food processor and blend until smooth.
4. Pour the egg mixture into the jars.
5. Cook the egg bites for 30 minutes, then remove from the oven and serve hot, or refrigerate for later.

Made famous by the global coffee chain Starbucks, these creamy little egg dishes are so easy to make if you have a steam oven! They're also packed with protein and can be dressed up beautifully for a special occasion. Add a handful of tri-color tomatoes or a quick fresh salsa and you've got breakfast worthy of company.

Feel free to add or change flavorings here. Fresh herbs, thinly sliced onion, roasted peppers, mushrooms or sundried tomatoes would make lovely inclusions. Put them into each jar or dish with the bacon.

I use small (4oz/125ml) jars for this recipe, but you can cook them in any small dish, bowl or jar. Egg bites can be made several days in advance and kept in the fridge. Eat them at room temperature, or reheat to the same temperature you cooked at just before serving.

Brunch Tarts

MAKES
4

PREP TIME
15 min

COOKING TIME
20 min

OVEN SETTINGS
400°F/200°C
Combination Steam
30% Humidity

INGREDIENTS

2 x 12 inch (30cm) square sheets frozen puff pastry, thawed and cut in half (quartered for the muffin pan version)
1 cup (50g) baby spinach
2 large field mushrooms, thickly sliced
4 slices streaky bacon
6 eggs, lightly beaten
Salt and pepper to season

METHOD

1. Preheat your oven to 400°F/200°C, Combination Steam, 30% humidity. Lightly grease four individual pie dishes or eight cups of a muffin pan.
2. Line baking dishes with pastry. Trim excess pastry if it doesn't fit, though a little overhang is fine as it'll puff and crisp at the edges. I usually have to cut a strip off one end - I lay it over the top of the filled tarts before baking; no one ever minds extra pastry!
3. Put a few spinach leaves and a couple of mushroom slices into the bottom of each tart. Season with salt and pepper, then carefully pour in enough beaten egg to almost fill. Lay a slice of bacon across the top (halve bacon if it's too long).
4. Bake the tarts until the filling is puffed and the pastry golden brown, about 20 minutes. Remove from the oven and leave to cool for five minutes before turning out. Serve hot or warm.

These will satisfy savory breakfast lovers on Christmas morning, without the fuss of a huge cooked breakfast. To save time, line the baking dishes, prepare fillings and even beat the eggs the day before, so all you have to do on Christmas morning is assemble and bake.

I make these in individual enamel pie dishes, but they also work well in a regular muffin pan. If you use a muffin pan you'll get eight small tarts instead of four larger ones - halve the ingredients for each one and drop the cooking time by a couple of minutes.

Quantities can be easily doubled or tripled if you're feeding a crowd.

French Toast For All

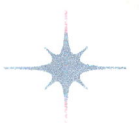

These two sandwiches are like French toast gone rogue, in the best possible way.

One savory and one sweet; take your pick! Or make both types and serve them as a Christmas morning brunch spread you'll be asked to repeat every year from here on out.

My preference when it comes to French toast is for bread that's got a good crust but a fluffy crumb. Don't bother with expensive sourdough here as the dense crumb won't soak up the egg mixture properly.

Increase and decrease ingredient quantities as you see fit, especially the eggs and milk, as different breads soak up different amounts of liquid.

If you want to prep ahead, assemble the sandwiches, dip and pan fry them, then put them into the fridge on your baking sheet. You can do this up to a few hours ahead of time; pop the sandwiches into your steam oven for the final cook just before you're ready to serve.

Cheese and Spinach French Toast Sandwiches

MAKES
4

PREP TIME
10 min

COOKING TIME
15 min

OVEN SETTINGS
400°F/200°C
Combination Steam
80% Humidity

INGREDIENTS

8 thick slices crusty white bread

1 garlic clove, cut in half

3 Tbsp Dijon mustard

1 1/2 cups (75g) baby spinach

7oz (200g) Gruyere or Fontina cheese, thickly sliced

6 eggs

1/2 cup whole milk

Salt and pepper for seasoning

2 Tbsp butter

METHOD

1. Preheat your oven to 400°F/200°C, Combination Steam, 80% humidity. Line a baking sheet with parchment (baking) paper.
2. Rub both sides of each slice of bread with the cut garlic, and spread half of the slices with mustard.
3. Put the cheese and spinach on the other slices of bread, and top with the mustard-spread slices.
4. Whisk the eggs and milk together in a wide, shallow dish which will fit a whole sandwich. Season with a little salt and pepper.
5. Place a large frying pan over medium high heat and add a little butter to coat the bottom.
6. While the pan heats, soak two of the sandwiches in the egg mix until it's absorbed enough to go right through the bread (but not so much it falls apart). You'll have to carefully turn them over to get both sides soaked. Transfer the soaked sandwiches straight into the fry pan and cook for a minute or two each side until browned. Don't worry about cooking through. Repeat with the remaining sandwiches, transferring the first two to the lined baking sheet once they're browned.
7. Transfer the remaining sandwiches to the baking sheet and cook until they're puffy, oozy and golden all over, about 10 minutes. Serve immediately.

These oozy, cheesy sandwiches are filling and so satisfying, and I love that they're meat free given there's so much ham and turkey around at this time of year!

If you want to make things really luxurious, pan fry sliced mushrooms in butter and add those to your sandwiches along with the spinach.

Choc Hazelnut and Strawberry French Toast Sandwiches

MAKES
4

PREP TIME
15 min

COOKING TIME
15 min

OVEN SETTINGS
400ºF/200ºC
Combination Steam
80% Humidity

INGREDIENTS

8 thick slices crusty white bread

7oz (200g) Nutella or other chocolate nut spread

8oz (240g) fresh strawberries, sliced

6 eggs

1/2 cup whole milk

1 Tbsp granulated sugar

Zest of 1 orange

2-3 Tbsp butter for the fry pan

METHOD

1. Preheat your oven to 400ºF/200ºC, Combination Steam, 80% humidity. Line a baking sheet with parchment (baking) paper.
2. Spread four slices of bread with the Nutella, then arrange the sliced strawberries on top. Top with the remaining slices of bread.
3. Whisk the eggs, milk, sugar and orange zest together in a wide, shallow dish which will fit a whole sandwich.
4. Place a large frying pan over medium high heat and add a little butter to coat the bottom.
5. While the pan heats, soak two of the sandwiches in the egg mix until it's absorbed enough to go right through the bread (but not so much it falls apart). You'll have to carefully turn them over to get both sides soaked. Transfer the soaked sandwiches straight into the fry pan and cook for a minute or two each side until browned. Don't worry about cooking through. Repeat with the remaining sandwiches, transferring the first two to the lined baking sheet once they're browned.
6. Transfer the remaining sandwiches to the baking sheet and cook until they're puffy, oozy and golden all over, about 10 minutes. Serve immediately.

The ubiquitous kids favorite spread, Nutella, gets a spin in these indulgent sandwiches stuffed with juicy berries. They're actually great at any time of year, but I think of them as a Christmas sandwich because they're such a special occasion breakfast.

There are a multitude of fillings you could substitute here. Think sliced bananas, other fresh berries, peanut butter or dulce de leche. If you prefer something with less sugar, replace Nutella with one of the healthier cacao or choc nut spreads available in the health food aisle of most supermarkets.

Starters

I love keeping Christmas dining casual but impressive.

In my family we don't do sit-down starters, preferring instead to have a few dishes which can be passed around while everyone chats and has a drink.

Easy to pick up and eat in a couple of bites, the dishes which follow are just right to begin any festive meal. All you'll need to worry about is who's pouring the drinks!

Roasted Pears with Prosciutto and Blue Cheese

Puff Pastry Cheese Straws

Three-Cheese Stuffed Mushrooms

Olive, Pesto and Cherry Tomato Tartlets

Pumpkin Dinner Rolls

Roasted Pears with Prosciutto and Blue Cheese

MAKES
16

PREP TIME
15 min

COOKING TIME
20 min

OVEN SETTINGS
400°F/200°C
Combination Steam
30% Humidity

INGREDIENTS

2 large pears, peeled, cored and cut into eighths

1 Tbsp extra virgin olive oil

Pepper to season

8 thin slices prosciutto

3ox (85g) gorgonzola dolce or other creamy blue cheese

16 baby arugula/rocket leaves, washed and dried well

METHOD

1. Preheat your oven to 400°F/200°C, Combination Steam, 30% humidity.
2. Toss the pears in the olive oil and spread over a baking tray. Season with pepper. Cook until they're soft and starting to brown at the edges, about 18-20 minutes. Remove and allow to cool. You can store the pears covered in the fridge for up to two days before using, if you like. Bring them to room temperature before proceeding with the recipe.
3. When you're ready to serve, lay the prosciutto slices out on a large board and cut each in half lengthways. Place an arugula/rocket leaf at the end of each piece of prosciutto, followed by a roasted pear wedge and a little cheese. Roll up to enclose the fillings in the prosciutto, and serve at room temperature.

I use roasted pears in all sorts of dishes: tossed through a green salad, piled into shortcrust pastry for a quick tart or served up as a side dish to roast chicken or pork. Here, they're used to create a simple little canape that's suitably festive but not too heavy.

Make sure your pears are relatively firm for this recipe. Very ripe fruit will collapse in the oven and you won't be able to create neat little canapes.

If you aren't a fan of blue cheese, thin slices of manchego or a very good aged parmesan are excellent substitutes.

Puff Pastry Cheese Straws

MAKES
16

PREP TIME
10 min

COOKING TIME
15 min

OVEN SETTINGS
375°F/190°C
Combination Steam
60% Humidity

INGREDIENTS

1 1/2 cups grated cheese mixed hard cheeses, I use a combination of parmesan and aged cheddar

1 sheet puff pastry all butter store bought, thawed but cold, measuring approximately 12in/30cm square

METHOD

1. Preheat your oven to 375°F/190°C, Combination Steam, 60% humidity. Line a baking sheet with parchment paper and set aside.
2. Scatter about a third of the cheese over your counter in a rectangle the size of your pastry sheet. Lay the pastry over the top and scatter another third of the cheese on top.
3. Roll out the pastry so it's about 1/8 inch (3mm) thick. This will press the cheese into each side as you flatten it.
4. Fold the pastry sheet in half and sprinkle with the remaining cheese, then roll again to make it 1/8 inch (3mm) thick. The dimensions don't matter too much, but do try to keep the pastry in a rectangle or square shape so it's easier to cut full straws from it.
5. Cut the pastry into strips about 1 inch (2.5cm) wide. Make them as long or short as you like; I prefer mine roughly 6-8 inches (15-20cm) long.
6. Transfer each strip to the prepared baking sheet. As you pick it up, twist the ends to make a long spiral. You may need to press the ends down onto the paper to stop them untwisting as you put each one down. Leave a gap of at least 1 inch (2.5cm) between each strip.
7. Chill the prepared straws for at least half an hour or up to a day before baking. Baking them from cold makes the pastry puff and separate much better than from room temperature.
8. Bake the straws until they're golden brown, puffed and flaky, about 15 minutes. Cool on the baking sheet and serve warm or at room temperature.

Puff pastry cheese straws, or twists, are such a great party snack. They come together fast and cook quickly, and they'll be the first thing to disappear off the appetizers plate!

I use a combination of parmesan and aged cheddar cheeses here; feel free to mix things up with different types of cheese. You need at least one fairly strong cheese so there's a good salty, cheesy hit to your pastry, so I wouldn't recommend very mild cheeses like mozzarella in this recipe.

Cheese straws can be assembled and refrigerated for up to a day, or frozen up to 2 months. Bake directly from the fridge or freezer, allowing a couple of extra minutes if frozen. The cheese straws are best served within a few hours of baking but they will keep, well sealed, for a day or two. Briefly warm them in a dry oven to refresh.

Three-Cheese Stuffed Mushrooms

MAKES
24

PREP TIME
25 min

COOKING TIME
15 min

OVEN SETTINGS
400°F/200°C
Combination Steam
50% Humidity

INGREDIENTS

24 (about 14oz/400g) button mushrooms
9oz (250g) ricotta cheese
1oz (30g) parmesan cheese, finely grated
1oz (30g) gorgonzola cheese
1 small clove garlic, minced
1 Tbsp chopped parsley leaves
2 tsp chopped thyme leaves
1/4 tsp ground black pepper
2 Tbsp olive oil

METHOD

1. Preheat your oven to 350°F/180°C, Combination Steam, 50% humidity. Line a baking sheet with parchment paper and set aside.
2. Remove the stems from the mushrooms and put the cups, upside down, on the baking sheet. Finely chop the stems.
3. Put the cheeses in a bowl and mash with a fork until combined. Add the mushroom stems, garlic, herbs and pepper. Stir well, then fill the mushroom cups with this mixture.
4. Drizzle with olive oil and cook until the mushrooms are softened and filling browned, about 15 minutes. Serve hot or warm.

Stuffed mushrooms seem to have fallen out of favor, but I love them. Savory and cheesy without being overly rich, these appetizer-sized mushroom bites are simple to make and the quantities can easily be doubled or tripled. If you can find them, use brown button mushrooms (Swiss Brown or Cremini). The flavor is a little deeper than with white mushrooms.

The mushrooms can be fully prepared up to 24 hours ahead and refrigerated, ready to pop in the oven just as your Christmas meal kicks off.

Olive, Pesto and Cherry Tomato Tartlets

MAKES
24

PREP TIME
20 min

COOKING TIME
12 min

OVEN SETTINGS
400°F/200°C
Combination Steam
50% Humidity

INGREDIENTS

2 x 12 inch (30cm) square sheets frozen puff pastry, thawed

2ox (55g) basil pesto

12 cherry or grape tomatoes, halved

24 kalamata olives, pitted

METHOD

1. Preheat your oven to 400°F/200°C, Combination Steam, 50% humidity. Lightly grease 2 x 12-cup patty pan trays and set aside.
2. Use an 8cm/3 inch cutter to cut 12 rounds from each sheet of pastry. Don't remove them from the sheet yet.
3. Spread a small amount of pesto over each pastry circle, leaving a 5mm/1/8 inch border around each one.
4. Put a cherry tomato half and an olive into each hole of the patty pan tray, then top with the pastry circles, pesto side down.
5. Cook until the pastry is puffed and golden brown, about 12 minutes. Remove from the oven, then carefully and quickly invert the tartlets onto a plate or serving tray.

Sometimes when you turn them out, a few of the tomatoes or olives might get left in the baking tray. Just pick them up gently (use a teaspoon if they're really hot), and pop them back on the tartlets. Serve hot or warm.

These little tarts are baked upside down, so the pastry gets maximum puff and browning during cooking.

You can prepare the tarts up to 12 hours ahead and store, unbaked, in the fridge. Once you bake them, they do need to be served fairly quickly.

Pumpkin Dinner Rolls

MAKES
16 rolls

PREP TIME
30 min plus 1 hr proofing time

COOKING TIME
20 min

OVEN SETTINGS
95°F/35°C
Steam 100% humidity
THEN
350°F/180°C
Combination Steam
30% Humidity

INGREDIENTS

1 cup (200g) pumpkin puree, at room temperature
1/4 cup (50g) granulated sugar
2 tsp fine salt
4 oz (120g) butter, softened
2 eggs
2 tsp active dry yeast (see note)
3/4 cup (185ml) milk, lukewarm
4 1/2 cups (600g) white bread flour

METHOD

Super soft and just a little sweet, these rolls serve double duty as either a starter or a side dish. Serve with lashings of salted butter for a low key but sophisticated start to a Christmas meal.

If you don't want to fuss with the string to shape your pumpkin rolls, make them as round rolls instead.

A note on yeast: I use active dried yeast. If you're using instant, skip the first step and just mix the yeast, milk and sugar straight in with the dough. It might take a little longer to complete the first proof if you use instant, anywhere up to 60 minutes.

1. Make the dough. Put all the ingredients into a large bowl and mix by hand or with a mixer until a soft, smooth and elastic dough forms. If you're mixing by hand this will take up to 10 minutes, in a mixer it takes around five minutes.
2. Place the dough in a clean bowl and set your oven to dough proofing (or steam, if you don't have a proofing setting), 100°F/38°C. Put the uncovered bowl in the oven until the dough has doubled in size, 30-40 minutes.
3. Turn the dough out onto a floured surface and gently press down to remove any large air pockets. Divide the dough into 16 pieces and form each into a smooth ball.
4. Optional step - if you want to make pumpkin shaped rolls: Take your string and cut 16 long pieces, about 24"/60cm each. Put a little vegetable or olive oil on your fingers and run each piece of string over them to lightly grease it. Place a piece of string over the middle of a formed roll, then turn it over and cross the string like you're wrapping a gift, and turn it back over again. Repeat so you have eight sections, then tie the string in a loose knot at the top and trim any excess. Don't pull the string too tight when you're wrapping it around the dough; you want it loose enough that it's not cutting into the dough because the rolls will expand later to create the pumpkin shape. Repeat the string tying for each roll.
5. Place the rolls on a lightly greased or parchment-lined 9 x 13 inch (22 x 32cm) pan. Set your oven once again to dough proofing (or steam, if you don't have a proofing setting), 100°F/38°C. Place the pan in the oven and let the rolls rise until they're puffed, 25-30 minutes.
6. With the pan still in the oven, change your oven settings to 350°F/180°C, Combination Steam, 30% humidity. Bake the rolls until they're golden brown, about 20 minutes, then remove from the oven and turn them onto a rack. Leave to cool for a few minutes then, if you've tied string around them, cut this off for serving.
7. Serve rolls warm or at room temperature. Store any leftovers in an airtight container for a couple of days at room temperature, or freeze for up to 2 months.

The Main Event

The following centerpiece dishes are worthy of any Christmas table.

They'll serve many, and can be mixed and matched for a beautiful multi-dish spread. Most of the hard work is done well ahead of time so you can get out of the kitchen faster. Just as we like it! After all, Christmas might be about the food, but it's just as much about the people we get to enjoy it with.

You'll also find a few delicious ways to use up your leftovers in this chapter, because there's not much better than making a whole new meal from a handful of fridge hangers-about!

Port and Redcurrant Glazed Ham

Christmas Roast Duck

Salmon with Maple Butter, Almonds and Dill Sauce

Whole Roasted Cauliflower with Moorish Spices

Turkey Breast Roll with Apricots and Walnuts

Sous Vide Turkey Breast with Herbs and Garlic

Classic Roast Turkey

Turkey Pot Pies

Turkey Salad with Vietnamese Dressing

Ham and Cheese Enchiladas

Port and Redcurrant Glazed Ham

SERVES
at least 12 as part of a banquet

PREP TIME
1 hour

COOKING TIME
1 hour

OVEN SETTINGS
340°F/170°C
Combination Steam
50% Humidity

INGREDIENTS

1 x 11lb (5kg) half-leg ham (shank end)

5.5oz (150g) redcurrant jelly

Juice 1 lemon

1/4 cup (60ml) port

Approximately 40 whole cloves

METHOD

1. Make the glaze. Put the jelly, lemon juice and 2 Tbsp water into a saucepan over medium heat. Cook until the jelly has melted and the mixture is smooth. Remove from heat, stir in the port and leave to cool.
2. Prepare the ham. Carefully cut through the skin around the top end of the shank. You can do this in a zig-zag decorative pattern, or just a straight cut. Starting from the cut, gently peel the skin back towards the widest part of the ham and remove, leaving the fat intact. Carefully score a diamond pattern into the fat with a small sharp knife. Be careful not to cut through into the flesh, as the fat will shrink back where it's cut too deeply.
3. Preheat your oven to 340°F/170°C, Combination Steam, 50% humidity. Place the ham into a large baking dish. Brush it all over with the glaze, then press one clove into the center of each diamond.
4. Cook the ham for one hour, basting with glaze every 15 minutes and turning it around in the oven if it's browning unevenly. At the end of cooking time, remove from the oven and rest for at least 20 minutes. You can serve the ham hot, warm or cold.

Glazing a ham using combi steam gives a burnished, glossy exterior and the juiciest texture I've ever been able to produce. Served with mustard, chutney and whichever sides take your fancy, it's an impressive but actually very easy main meal.

Depending on the size of your oven, you may not fit an entire leg of ham in it. Don't let that stop you. A half-leg, like we're doing here, is perfectly acceptable and the leftovers won't take up as much space in the fridge.

If you're preparing ahead (I really recommend it here), the ham can be fully glazed and cooked up to 3 days ahead of time. Store it in the fridge, covered with a damp kitchen towel, until an hour before you want to carve and serve it.

Christmas Roast Duck

SERVES
6-8 as part of a banquet

PREP TIME
20 min

COOKING TIME
50 min

OVEN SETTINGS
340°F/170°C
Combination Steam
50% Humidity
THEN
Fan Forced/Convection
450°F/230°C

INGREDIENTS

1 x 4.5lb (2.1kg) whole duck
1 1/2 tsp flaky sea salt
1 1/2 tsp ground cinnamon
2 sprigs rosemary
1 orange, chopped into a few pieces

METHOD

1. Preheat your oven to 340°F/170°C, Combination Steam, 50% humidity.
2. Rinse the cavity of the duck and pat dry all over with paper towels. If your duck came in a sweaty plastic bag I'd recommend doing this the day before, or at least a few hours out, and returning it, uncovered, to the fridge so it can dry out a little.
3. Sprinkle a little of the salt inside the cavity then rub the rest of the salt and the cinnamon over the skin. Put the rosemary and orange pieces into the cavity. Don't be tempted to stuff too much orange in there, you need enough free space for heat to circulate. To help the fat render out during cooking, use a skewer to poke several holes into the fattiest parts of the skin around the cavity, neck and thighs.
4. Set the duck on a rack or perforated pan over a baking dish and put it on the middle shelf of the oven. Cook for 50 minutes.
5. Change oven setting to 450°F/230°C, fan forced/convection (no steam). Take the duck out of the oven and give it a quick baste with the rendered fat, then cook until golden and crispy and the juices run clear when tested with a skewer, about 10-15 minutes.
6. Rest the duck in a warm place for at least 20 minutes before carving. If you want to hold it for longer, cover with foil to help retain the heat (see note about crispy skin). It's perfectly acceptable to serve this at a warm room temperature, in which case you could leave it to rest for anywhere up to an hour and a half before carving.

In Australia Christmas equals cherry season, which is great news as far as duck is concerned because they're a fantastic pairing! Cherries have a vibrance and tartness which goes so well with rich duck meat. Simply pitted and tossed in a little orange juice is my favorite way to serve them.

If you're celebrating in the Northern hemisphere's wintery depths, serve your duck with a composed salad of mandarin/clementine segments, flat leaf parsley and finely sliced red onion.

If you have a temperature probe for cooking in your steam oven, definitely use it here. The meat should cook to an internal temperature of 165°F/75°C.

After it's rested, you may find the duck skin is less than crispy. If so, pop it back into a blistering hot oven - 450°F/230°C - for no more than 5 minutes, just before serving. You don't want to cook the meat any further or ruin all that lovely resting you've done, so as soon as the skin starts to sizzle again, take it out.

Salmon with Maple Butter, Almonds and Dill Sauce

SERVES
8 as part of a banquet

PREP TIME
30 min

COOKING TIME
45 min
(15 minutes at higher temp)

OVEN SETTINGS
125°F/52°C
Steam or Sous Vide Setting
100% humidity
OR
185°F/85°C
Steam 100% humidity

INGREDIENTS

Salmon
2.4 lb (1.2kg) salmon side (skin on, bones removed)
2 tsp flaky salt (or 1 tsp fine salt)
1 tsp black pepper
Maple Butter
4oz (120g) unsalted butter, softened
⅓ cup (80ml) maple syrup (real maple, not imitation!)
1 clove garlic, minced
Lemon and Dill Sauce
1 cup (250ml) sour cream, full fat (or creme fraiche)
1/3 cup fresh dill, finely chopped
1 small shallot, very finely chopped
2 lemons, finely zested
1/2 tsp flaky salt
To serve
3 lemons, cut into 'cheeks'
1 cup (120g) flaked almonds, toasted

METHOD

1. Mix lemon and dill sauce ingredients in a bowl until smooth, then set aside. You can do this up to 24 hours ahead and store in the fridge, just bring it to room temperature for serving.
2. Preheat your oven to 125°F/52°C, Steam or Sous Vide Setting, 100% humidity (see notes above for alternative temperature and time if your oven doesn't cook this low).
3. Line a perforated baking sheet with parchment paper and set this over a solid pan to catch any juices. Put the salmon, skin side down, onto the baking sheet and rub with salt and pepper. Put in the oven and cook for 45 minutes.

This is a luxurious centerpiece meal, and cooking the salmon at such a low (and specific) temperature means you get silky, flaky fish that's super moist and perfectly cooked from edge to edge.

Try to get a side of salmon in one piece for this dish. Don't panic about an exact weight; if it weighs 25% more or less than the given weight, the cooking time remains the same. You may want to 1.5x the maple butter and dill sauce if you have a lot of extra fish. If you can't get a whole side of salmon, you can cook this in individual portions. In that case, cook salmon filets for 35-45 minutes.

If your steam oven isn't reliable at low temperatures (ie if it doesn't have a sous vide setting), don't muck around with food safety or doneness. It's a costly mistake if things go wrong, not to mention your guests won't thank you for food poisoning! Instead, preheat your oven using the steam setting and cook the salmon at 185°F/85°C for 15 minutes per inch of thickness (I'm talking about the thickest part in the middle of the filet). Scale that time up or down by a few minutes for a thinner or thicker piece. The texture is a little different and more flaky than the low temp version but it's still excellent.

I like to serve this at room temperature. If you need to cook ahead of time, cook no more than 12 hours out and chill the salmon, undressed, immediately after cooking. Bring to room temperature to serve and dress just before you put it on the table.

METHOD Continued...

4. Make the maple butter. While the salmon cooks, place the butter in a saucepan over medium high heat. It will melt, then foam, and then the solids in the butter will begin to turn brown. The browning happens very quickly so don't take your eyes off it once the foaming starts! When the butter browns, remove from heat immediately and add the maple syrup and garlic. Stir to combine then set aside.
5. Grill the lemons. Heat a griddle pan or barbecue plate until very hot, then put the cut sides of the lemons down until they're blackened and caramelized. Remove and set aside.
6. When the salmon is done, use the parchment paper to transfer it to a serving dish. Carefully slide the paper out from underneath, leaving any juices around the fish. If preparing ahead, refrigerate at this point.
7. If serving immediately, pour the warm maple butter over the salmon. Dollop the lemon and dill sauce thickly over the top, then scatter with the toasted almonds. Serve, cut into slices, with plenty of the juices and butter from the serving dish. Offer the charred lemon for squeezing over the top.

Whole Roasted Cauliflower with Moorish Spices

SERVES
8 as part of a banquet

PREP TIME
20 min

COOKING TIME
35 min

OVEN SETTINGS
200°F/400°C
Combination Steam
50% Humidity

INGREDIENTS

1 whole cauliflower, outer leaves trimmed off
2 Tbsp olive oil
1/2 tsp fine salt
1/2 tsp ground black pepper
2 tsp paprika
1 tsp ground turmeric
1 tsp ground coriander
1 tsp ground cumin
1 clove garlic, minced
Zest and juice of 1 lemon, plus zest of 1 extra lemon for serving
1 x 7oz (200g) tub hummus dip, or natural unsweetened yogurt
1/4 cup (50g) toasted flaked almonds
1/4 cup (45g) dried apricots, sliced
A large handful fresh mint leaves, for serving

METHOD

1. Preheat your oven to 400°F/200°C, Combination Steam, 50% humidity.
2. Mix the oil, salt, pepper, spices, garlic, lemon zest and juice in a small bowl. Rub this mixture all over the cauliflower to cover. Put the cauliflower into a roasting dish and cook until it's well browned on the outside and just soft in the middle, about 35 minutes.
3. To serve, spread the dip or yogurt on a serving platter. Top with the hot or warm cooked cauliflower and sprinkle with the almonds, apricots, mint and extra lemon zest just before bringing to the table. Serve hot or warm, sliced into chunky wedges.

If you need to impress non-meat-eaters at the Christmas table, this is your dish. It's equally at home as a vegetarian main as it is a substantial side to meat dishes, so everyone wins.

This recipe boasts a seemingly huge list of ingredients. It is lengthy, but most are supermarket staples, and the preparation is relatively quick.

You can mix the spice rub, coat the cauliflower and set it aside for up to a few hours before cooking.

All Things Turkey

For most people, it wouldn't be Christmas without a turkey roast. These are my top three: one simple, one fancy stuffed roast and one classic full-bird. Take your pick!

Turkey Breast Roll with Apricots and Walnuts

SERVES
8-12 as part of a banquet

PREP TIME
1 hour

COOKING TIME
1 hour 15 min

OVEN SETTINGS
375°F/190°C
Combination Steam
30% Humidity

INGREDIENTS

2 Tbsp olive oil

4 slices stale white bread, cut into 1/2 inch (1cm) cubes

1 clove garlic, minced

1 medium brown onion, chopped

6 slices pancetta, chopped

1/2 cup (85g) dried apricots, finely chopped

1/2 cup (70g) walnuts, toasted and finely chopped

1/3 cup (80ml) light chicken stock

1 x 4.5 lb (2kg) boneless turkey breast, skin on

2 Tbsp butter, very soft

A boneless stuffed turkey breast is easier to cook and serve than the traditional whole roast bird, and it will cook more evenly, too.

A meat probe or instant-read thermometer is very handy for stuffed roasts as it's the most accurate way to check whether everything is cooked through. The internal temperature of the roast should reach 165°F/74°C. If you don't have a thermometer, you can cook according to the stuffed weight of the roast. In a combi steam oven, it'll take approximately 15 minutes per pound (450g).

METHOD

1. Make the stuffing. Heat half the oil in a frypan over medium heat, and fry the bread until it's crispy and golden. Remove the bread and set aside. Return the pan to heat with the remaining oil and cook the garlic, onion and pancetta, stirring, until the onions are just beginning to brown. Stir in the apricots, then return the bread to the pan with the walnuts and stock. Give it all a stir and season liberally with black pepper. Chill until completely cold.

2. Preheat your oven to 375°F/190°C, Combination Steam setting, 30% humidity. Lay the turkey out on a large board, skin side down. Carefully cut a flap in the thickest part of the meat and open it out, then use a meat mallet to flatten everything to about an inch (2.5cm) thick.

3. Pile the stuffing lengthwise down the center of the meat, leaving a little space at the ends. Lift the pointed end and sides to enclose the stuffing. Secure with toothpicks, then lift the flap end and secure with more toothpicks. Turn the roast over and tie bakers twine at 1 inch (2.5cm) intervals to secure. Remove the toothpicks after you've done this, as they've done their job and you don't want to cut through them later on.

4. Cook the roast. Place stuffed roast in a baking dish. Rub with the butter and season well with salt and pepper. Cook until the center of the roast reads 165°F/74°C on a thermometer, about 1 hour 15 minutes. A couple of times during cooking, baste the roast with pan juices.

5. Remove the cooked roast from the oven and leave to rest in a warm place. If you'd like to make gravy with the pan juices, take the turkey out and wrap loosely in aluminum foil while you do this. Cut into thick slices and serve hot or warm.

Sous Vide Turkey Breast with Herbs and Garlic

SERVES
6-8 as part of a banquet

PREP TIME
10 min

COOKING TIME
3 hours 15 min plus chilling time 12 hours

OVEN SETTINGS
150°F/65°C
Steam
100% Humidity
THEN
High heat grill/broiler

INGREDIENTS

For cooking the meat

1 x 4.5lb (2kg) single, boneless turkey breast, skin on

3/4 tsp fine salt

2 sprigs rosemary

2 sprigs thyme

5 sage leaves

3 cloves garlic, bruised, skin on is fine

To finish

4 oz (120g) unsalted butter, softened

1/2 tsp fine salt

1/2 tsp black pepper

METHOD

1. Prepare the meat and chill overnight. Rub salt all over the underside and under the skin of the turkey (you can loosen the skin by carefully sliding your fingers underneath, then sprinkle salt in there and rub it all over before smoothing the skin back over the meat nicely).
2. Put the salted meat into a vacuum bag with the herbs and garlic tucked underneath, and seal (see notes if you don't have a vacuum sealer).
3. Return the turkey to the fridge for the flavors to infuse, for anywhere from 12 to 24 hours.
4. Cook the turkey. When you're ready to cook, preheat your oven to 150°F/65°C, Steam, 100% humidity.
5. Put the bagged meat onto a perforated pan or directly onto the oven rack and cook for 3 hours.
6. While the turkey is cooking, mix the butter, salt and pepper in a small bowl and set aside.

For smaller holiday gatherings, or those where you want more than one meat centerpiece, try this simple turkey breast. It's easy to cook and carve, with incredibly juicy meat and crispy golden skin.

Your steam oven will need to be capable of cooking at low temperatures for this dish.

Do NOT buy a brined turkey breast (most frozen supermarket turkey is brined, so check carefully). The salting and seasoning of the meat in the recipe takes care of this; if you do it to an already brined piece of meat it'll come out far too salty.

If you don't have a vacuum sealing machine, double layered zip-lock bags will work for this recipe. Although you can do 'bagless' sous vide cooking in a steam oven, I do recommend you bag the meat and seasonings for this particular dish. It will allow the seasonings to penetrate the meat better. To do the zip-lock bag option, put the filled bags into a large container of cold water. Let the water come up almost to the sealing strips of the bags to displace the air. Close the inner bag's seal first, then the outer one and remove from the water.

METHOD Continued...

7. At the end of cooking, remove the turkey from the oven and cut open the bag. Discard the herbs and garlic but keep any cooking juices.
8. Crisp the skin and serve. Preheat a broiler/grill to high heat. While it heats, put the turkey, skin side up, into a baking dish with the cooking juices poured around it.
9. Smear the butter over the turkey skin (all of it! I know it looks like too much but trust me). Broil/grill until it's golden brown. The butter will melt off into the pan fairly quickly, likely before you even get it under the broiler. Don't worry. Baste the turkey with the melted butter and pan juices frequently until it reaches the color you're looking for. If you find there are spots getting too browned, just cover those bits with a little foil while the rest of the skin catches up.
10. Rest the turkey in a warm place for 20-30 minutes, then carve into slices for serving, with some of the buttery pan juices drizzled over the top. Leftovers, if you're lucky enough to have any, will be tender and succulent enough to eat cold the next day.

Classic Roast Turkey

SERVES
8-10 as part of a banquet

PREP TIME
15 min

COOKING TIME
2 hours 10 min plus 30 min resting time

OVEN SETTINGS
185°F/85°C
Steam
100% Humidity

THEN
350°F/180°C
Convection
No Steam

INGREDIENTS

1 x 9lb (4kg) whole fresh turkey, giblets and neck removed,

1 Tbsp fine salt

4 Tbsp butter, softened

3/4 cup (185ml) maple syrup (use the real stuff, no imitation maple here please)

2 Tbsp Dijon mustard

1 Tbsp apple cider vinegar

1/2 tsp garlic powder

1 tsp smoked paprika

1/2 tsp cayenne pepper (optional, if you'd like a gentle hum in your glaze)

METHOD

1. Prepare the turkey. Pat the skin dry with paper towel, then rub all over the outside and the interior cavity with salt. I use approximately a tablespoon's worth of fine salt for this – you want enough to rub all over every part of the bird. Tie the ends of the legs together with kitchen string, then tuck the wings under the body and use another piece of string to tie right around the turkey, securing the wings close to the body (see photograph for example). The 'wing string' is optional, but it stops the possibility of the wing ends popping out from under the bird during roasting and keeps it all looking nice and neat.
2. Steam the turkey. Put the prepared turkey on a wire rack or perforated tray, with a solid pan underneath to catch any juices and fat. Put the turkey into the oven and set it to 185°F/85°C, Steam, 100% humidity (a cold start is fine here). Cook for 40 minutes.
3. Make the glaze. While the turkey is steaming, mix together the maple syrup, mustard, vinegar, garlic, smoked paprika and cayenne pepper. Set aside.

This is my favorite way to roast turkey in a steam oven, by gently steaming it and then finishing with a hot, dry heat to cook through and crisp the skin.

Although you could do this dish with a frozen supermarket turkey, I prefer a free range or organic pasture raised bird. It will have far more flavor than a mass-produced turkey (not to mention the animal welfare benefits).

You'll note the recipe calls for a relatively small turkey. That's intentional: partly because many steam ovens are compact models which can't accommodate a giant 20lb bird, but also because the larger the turkey is, the harder it is to cook evenly! This is true no matter what method you choose. If you do want to go larger, you can fit up to about a 15lb/7kg turkey into even a compact steam oven, which is plenty for most families. Beyond that you'll need a full sized steam oven. You'll have to adjust cooking times accordingly with a larger turkey to achieve the correct internal temperature. For a very large bird weighing more than 15lb/7kg, increase the steaming time to 1 hour instead of the 40 minutes specified below.

METHOD Continued...

4. Roast the turkey. At the end of the steaming time, remove the turkey from the oven (it won't look or smell very appealing at this point; stay with me, because things are going to get a whole lot better soon). Change your oven setting to 350°F/180°C, Convection (no steam), or switch to your regular oven if your steam oven doesn't have standard oven capabilities. If you have a second oven with a pyrolytic/self cleaning function rather than a steam cleaning function, I'd recommend you switch ovens at this point anyway. Pyrolytic clean is going to make your clean-up job much easier.
5. Rub the steamed turkey all over with the softened butter, and put it back in the oven. Roast for 30 minutes, then brush with the glaze and continue roasting, brushing with more glaze every 15 minutes, until the thickest part of the bird, in the leg meat just next to the breast, reaches 163-169°F (73-76°C) on an instant read thermometer. If you don't have a thermometer, test the leg meat with a skewer; the juices should run almost clear. The roasting part of cooking should take somewhere between 1 1/2-2 hours. If the turkey is browning too quickly, cover it with a tented piece of foil to protect the skin. If the juices are starting to burn in the pan underneath the bird, add a half cup of water and check regularly to see if it needs more.
6. Remove the cooked bird from the oven and place it somewhere warm to rest for 30 minutes. I cover the turkey with a sheet of baking paper and a dish towel, which will keep the heat in but allow some air-flow.
7. You're done! Present your beautiful turkey to the waiting crowd and, if you're like me, hand off carving duties to someone else while you enjoy a glass of wine.

Leftover But Not Left Out

Don't let your leftovers become sad and sorry in the fridge. Instead, turn them into one of these gorgeous creations and you'll have a whole new meal for those hazy, lazy post-Christmas days when no one wants to leave the house for a grocery run!

Turkey Pot Pies

SERVES
6

PREP TIME
15 min

COOKING TIME
20 min

OVEN SETTINGS
400°F/200°C
Combination Steam
50% Humidity

INGREDIENTS

3 Tbsp butter
1 leek, finely sliced (or 1 medium onion, diced)
1/3 cup (50g) all-purpose (plain) flour
1 cup (250ml) chicken stock
1 cup (250ml) whole milk (or cream)
1 1/2 cups (200g) leftover roasted vegetables, roughly chopped
3 cups (400g) cooked turkey, roughly chopped
10oz (300g) all-butter puff pastry I use one which comes in a pre-rolled sheet for ease)
1 egg

These savory and creamy pies are the perfect way to use leftover roasted turkey and vegetables, and baking them using combi steam means the pastry will be flaky, puffy and sky high.

I used leftover roasted potatoes, pumpkin and carrots for the pictured pies. The vegetables were lightly oiled and seasoned with mixed herbs before roasting; if you aren't using pre-seasoned vegetables you may wish to add a little thyme, rosemary or oregano to the sauce.

You do not have to make your own puff pastry for this recipe, but I would recommend buying an all-butter pre-made puff, rather than a vegetable-fat-based one. It'll be more flaky and crisp, and taste amazing.

METHOD

1. Preheat your oven to 400°F/200°C, Combination Steam, 50% humidity. Lightly grease the inside of 6 x 12oz/1 1/2 cup ramekins, or a single 8 cup baking dish. Set aside.
2. Heat the butter in a saucepan over medium heat. Add the leek and cook, stirring often, until very soft, about five minutes. Add the flour to the pan and cook for a further 2 minutes, stirring constantly.
3. Whisk in the chicken stock and milk, a little at a time. Whisk well after each addition until the mixture smooths out. It'll be very thick to start with, but will loosen as you add more liquid. When all the liquid has been added, bring to a boil over medium heat, stirring constantly. Simmer until the mixture thickens enough to coat the back of a spoon, then remove from heat. Stir in turkey, then fold through the roasted vegetables. Add salt and pepper to taste.
4. Fill the prepared ramekins or dish with the turkey filling. Lightly beat the egg with a tablespoon of water in a small bowl, and set aside.
5. Cover the top of the dish/es with the puff pastry. It should hang a half inch (1cm) over the edges of the dish/es, to allow for a good lid which covers the entire top of the pie. Trim excess with a sharp knife. Cut a decorative shape for the top of each pie from any pastry scraps.
6. Brush the pastry all over with egg wash, then cut a few slits in the top to allow steam to escape.
7. Put the pie/s onto a sheet pan in case they spill over in the oven, and cook until the filling is bubbling and the pastry is puffed and golden brown, about 20 minutes for individual pies or 30 minutes for a larger pie.
8. Serve individual pies directly in the baking dishes. For a large pie, cut through the pastry with a serrated knife to make neat portions, then scoop the filling and pastry onto warmed plates.

Turkey Salad with Vietnamese Dressing

SERVES
4

PREP TIME
20 min

COOKING TIME
none

OVEN SETTINGS
400°F/200°C
Combination Steam
50% Humidity

INGREDIENTS

For the dressing

1 clove garlic, minced

1 red chili, minced (de-seed if you don't like things too spicy)

2 limes, juiced (or more to taste)

2 Tbsp granulated sugar

3 Tbsp fish sauce (or more to taste)

For the salad

1lb (450g) cold cooked turkey, cut or shredded into bite sized pieces

7oz (200g) dried rice vermicelli noodles

2 cups (200g) bean sprouts

1 cucumber, peeled and sliced

1 red bell pepper (capsicum), de-seeded and sliced

3 scallions, finely sliced

2 tsp sesame oil

1 bunch fresh cilantro (coriander), leaves picked

1 bunch fresh mint, leaves picked

1/3 cup (55g) roasted peanuts, chopped

METHOD

1. Mix all the dressing ingredients together in a bowl. Mix in 1/4 cup water and taste to check the balance of salty, sour and sweet. Add more lime juice or fish sauce to taste if necessary.
2. Prepare the noodles according to packet directions (the ones I use just need a 5-10 minute soak in boiling water, then a rinse in cold water). Drain well and cut into shorter lengths if they seem too long.
3. Mix half of the dressing with the turkey and set aside while you assemble the other ingredients.
4. Put the drained noodles, bean sprouts, cucumber, bell pepper and scallions into a bowl with the dressed turkey and the sesame oil. Toss to combine, then taste and add more dressing as required.
5. Mix through the herbs, then pile the salad onto a serving platter. Scatter the nuts over the top and serve immediately.

Got leftover cooked turkey but tired of rich, hot meals? Turn your meat into this fresh, punchy and substantial salad with rice noodles, vegetables and my favorite Vietnamese chili and lime dressing.

Ham and Cheese Enchiladas

SERVES
4

PREP TIME
10 min

COOKING TIME
20 min

OVEN SETTINGS
350ºF/180ºC
Combination Steam
30% Humidity

INGREDIENTS

3 cups (250g) chopped cooked ham
1 cup (250ml) sour cream
4 Tbsp pickled jalapeno chiles, finely chopped
3 scallions, finely sliced
2 1/2 cups (250g) shredded Cheddar cheese
8 large soft flour tortillas
1 x 10 oz jar (280g) store-bought enchilada sauce
2 tomatoes, deseeded and chopped
1 bunch cilantro (coriander), leaves picked

METHOD

1. Heat oven to 350°F/180°C, Combination Steam, 30% humidity. Lightly grease a 13x9 inch (33x23cm) baking dish.
2. Mix the ham, sour cream, jalapenos, scallions and 2 cups of the cheese in a large bowl.
3. Divide the ham mixture evenly onto each tortilla, spreading it out so it covers about half of the surface. Roll each one up and place seam-side down in the baking dish.
4. Pour enchilada sauce over the tortillas and sprinkle with the remaining cheese.
5. Bake until the cheese is golden and the filling thoroughly heated, about 20 minutes. Remove from the oven and serve on warmed plates, with tomato and cilantro leaves scattered over the top.

This is what you make when you're tired of ham in sandwiches, salads and quiche! A spicy, cheesy, Tex-Mex style dinner that's in no way refined but in every way delicious. Combi steam makes the dish cook faster, and keeps the filling oozy and creamy.

If you're serving this to kids you may want to skip the jalapenos, or serve them on the side.

Sides

I think I almost like the sides more than the big, celebrated Christmas roasts on a festive table.

These are a few of my all-time favorites, from salad to stuffing and everything in between. They're not difficult to make but are a little more celebration-worthy than plain steamed or roasted vegetables.

Crispy Roasted Potatoes

Steam Oven Mashed Potatoes

Green Beans with Almonds

Carrots, Ricotta and Lemon

Christmas Rice Salad

Brussels Sprouts and Couscous Salad

Bacon Wrapped Sausages

Sour Cherry and Pecan Stuffing

Crispy Roasted Potatoes

SERVES
8 as part of a banquet

PREP TIME
10 min

COOKING TIME
1 hr 20 min

OVEN SETTINGS
212°F/100°C
Steam
100% Humidity

THEN
350°F/180°C
Convection
No Steam

INGREDIENTS

2 lb floury potatoes
1/2 cup olive oil (or duck fat)
2 teaspoons fine salt

METHOD

1. Steam the potatoes. Preheat your oven to 212°F/100°C, Steam, 100% humidity.
2. Peel your potatoes if you want to (although you certainly don't have to - I actually love a roasted potato with skin!). Depending on the size, cut them into halves or quarters. You want each piece to be roughly 1.5-2 inches (4-5cm) in diameter.
3. Arrange the potatoes in a single layer in a stainless steel pan and put the pan into your oven. Steam until they're tender when pierced with a knife, about 30 minutes.
4. Roast the potatoes. Remove the steamed potatoes from the oven and change the setting to 350°F/180°C, Convection/Fan Forced (no steam). While the oven heats, drain the potatoes of any water and return them to the tray. Give them a good shake around to crush the edges slightly, this will help make them extra crispy later.
5. Pour the oil or duck fat over the shaken-around potatoes and season with salt. Toss to make sure the potatoes are well coated.
6. Return the pan to the hot oven and roast the potatoes for 45 minutes to an hour, until they're golden, crisp and crunchy on the outside. Give them a stir towards the end of cooking, but don't be tempted to do so until they've formed a really good crust, or you'll lose all the crunchy bits to the bottom of the pan!
7. Season the potatoes with extra flaky salt, then pile them into a warmed bowl and serve.

The best roasted potatoes are a two-step affair, but you can use your steam oven to make the first step easier! Steamed and then roasted, your potatoes will be impossibly tender inside and shatteringly crisp outside.

Duck fat potatoes are a really special treat for Christmas. Use it in place of the olive oil for an amazing, savory depth of flavor and crunchy texture.

Floury potatoes are key here. You want Russets in the USA; Sebago in Australia; or Maris Piper in the UK.

I prefer to make these on the day of serving. You can make and keep them warm in a dry oven for up to a couple of hours before serving.

Steam Oven Mashed Potatoes

SERVES
8 as part of a banquet

PREP TIME
10 min

COOKING TIME
25 min

OVEN SETTINGS
212°F/100°C
Steam
100% Humidity

INGREDIENTS

3lb (1.5kg) floury potatoes, peeled, halved and cut into 1 inch (2.5cm) thick slices
1 tsp salt
4 Tbsp unsalted butter, at room temperature
1/3 cup milk or cream, warmed
1/2 tsp salt (optional, to taste)
3 Tbsp unsalted butter, extra, melted
1/2 bunch chives, chopped

METHOD

1. Put potatoes into a lightweight stainless steel pan and season with salt. Put into your cold oven and set to 212°F/100°C, Steam (100% humidity). Cook for 25-30 minutes or until the potatoes are very soft. You should be able to easily break them with the back of a spoon.
2. When the potatoes are cooked, drain off any excess water and tip them into a deep bowl or pan.
3. Add the diced butter and milk (or cream), then mash well. If your mash is too stiff, add a couple of extra tablespoons of warmed milk. Season with extra salt if necessary.
4. Transfer to a serving bowl and drizzle the mash with melted butter. Sprinkle with chives and serve hot.

Steamed potatoes make the best mash, and this is my go-to recipe. It's simple, no fuss and works every single time, without the mess of boiling starchy potato water.

Floury and all rounder potatoes work best for mash. In Australia, Sebago are perfect all rounders. In the USA, Russets are a great choice, and in the UK I'd use Maris Pipers.

Please, please, for the love of all that is good and potato-y, DO NOT use a whisk, stick blender, food processor or blender for this recipe. A low-tech hand held potato masher is all you need. Mashed potatoes will quickly go from perfect and creamy to gluey and tough using appliances.

Want that incredibly silky smooth mash you get in restaurants? It can be done if you care enough to make extra effort! To make silky restaurant potatoes, push your finished mash through a sieve to get out any chunks. You may also want to double or even triple the amount of butter you use (yes, that's why restaurant mash tastes so amazing!).

Keeping mash warm is easy when you have a steam oven. Before you garnish, pop the entire serving bowl into your oven at 175°F/80°C, Steam, 80% humidity. It'll keep like that for a good couple of hours, just take out and garnish to serve. Need to reheat? Same thing, although you may wish to raise the temp to 195°F/90°C so they don't take so long to heat through. I like to give the potatoes a good stir after reheating to make sure the consistency is even.

Green Beans with Almonds

SERVES
8 as part of a banquet

PREP TIME
15 min

COOKING TIME
12 min

OVEN SETTINGS
212°F/100°C
Steam
100% Humidity

INGREDIENTS

1lb 10oz (750g) fresh green beans, washed and topped (I leave the tails on for presentation)

7oz (200g) whole almonds, roasted

3 Tbsp balsamic vinegar

2 Tbsp extra virgin olive oil

Coarsely ground black pepper to taste

METHOD

1. Preheat your oven to 212°F/100°C, Steam, 100% humidity.
2. Put the beans into a large stainless steel pan and steam until soft but with a little bite, about 12 minutes.
3. While the beans cook, whisk together the oil and vinegar and add black pepper to taste. Set aside.
4. Once the beans are cooked to your liking, remove from the oven and toss in the dressing while hot, so they absorb the flavors. Pile them onto a platter and scatter the almonds over the top to serve.

With these beans, I like a dressing that leans towards too vinegary. I know that's not for everyone, so feel free to increase the oil to taste. I don't add salt because almost everything else we eat with this dish is salty enough. The counterpoint of something vibrant and tart is refreshing.

You can serve these hot or at room temperature. If you're eating leftovers the next day I would serve at room temp, as heating the dressed beans makes them taste unpleasant.

Carrots, Ricotta and Lemon

SERVES
8 as part of a banquet

PREP TIME
20 min

COOKING TIME
20 min

OVEN SETTINGS
400°F/200°C
Combination Steam
60% Humidity

INGREDIENTS

2.2lb (1kg) baby carrots, peeled and halved lengthwise

Zest and juice of 2 lemons

2 tsp clear honey

1 Tbsp extra virgin olive oil

Salt to taste

7oz (200g) firm ricotta cheese, crumbled

1 bunch parsley, leaves roughly chopped

METHOD

1. Preheat your oven to 400°F/200°C, Combination Steam, 60% humidity.
2. Line a baking sheet with parchment paper and spread the carrots out in a single layer (no oil necessary!). Don't overcrowd the carrots: if your baking sheet isn't very large, you may wish to use two. Cook until the carrots are tender and beginning to blacken at the edges, about 20 minutes.
3. While the carrots cook, whisk the lemon zest and juice, honey, oil and salt together and set aside.
4. Arrange the cooked carrots on a serving platter and spoon over the dressing. Scatter ricotta and parsley over the top and serve warm or at room temperature.

This is one of those simple side dishes which seems to win with everyone, and almost every time I make it I get asked for the recipe. Make more than you need, because you'll probably find the serving plate completely bare by the time second helpings come around.

When buying ricotta cheese, try to get the firm variety which is cut from a wheel, rather than the very soft tub variety. If the tub version is all you can find, drain it in a fine sieve overnight before using.

I use baby carrots because they're sweeter and more tender, not to mention very pretty on the plate. Regular carrots are absolutely fine as a replacement.
Although I think it's best warm, I've been known to eat the leftovers of this dish straight from the fridge the next day.

Christmas Rice Salad

 **SERVES** 8-10 as part of a banquet	 **PREP TIME** 20 min	**COOKING TIME** 40 min	 OVEN SETTINGS 212°F/100°C Steam 100% Humidity

INGREDIENTS

2 cups (400g) medium grain brown rice

1/2 cup (100g) black rice (if you can't find it, increase the quantity of brown rice)

1/3 cup (85ml) extra virgin olive oil

1/3 cup (85ml) rice wine vinegar (apple cider vinegar is a good substitute)

Zest and juice of 1 lemon

1 Tbsp harissa paste (or 1-2 minced garlic cloves plus 1 minced red chili pepper)

2/3 cup (100g) dried cranberries, roughly chopped

1 large bunch parsley, leaves picked and roughly chopped

1 large bunch mint, leaves picked and roughly chopped

1/2 cup (50g) shelled pistachio nuts, roughly chopped

3 1/2oz (100g) Persian feta cheese, crumbled

METHOD

1. Mix the rice with 4 cups (1 litre) cold water in a shallow stainless steel tray. Put in your steam oven and set to 212°F/100°C, Steam, 100% humidity. Cook for 40-45 minutes, or until the rice has absorbed the water and is cooked through. Fluff the rice with a fork and set aside while you get the dressing ready.
2. Make the dressing. Whisk the oil, vinegar, lemon zest and juice and harissa paste in a small bowl.
3. Put the warm rice into a mixing bowl. Pour the dressing over and mix well to combine. Let the rice cool to room temperature (if you'd like to hold off serving for a while, cover the bowl at this point and put in the fridge until about 20 minutes before you're ready to serve).
4. When you're ready to serve the salad, add the cranberries and herbs to the rice mixture and stir to combine. Put into a serving bowl or spread onto a platter and scatter the nuts and feta cheese over the top. Serve at room temperature.

Despite the name, this salad is a mainstay at all times of the year in my house! It's often requested for potluck dinners and barbecues, so don't keep it just for Christmas.

Don't shy away from the quantity of herbs in the recipe. You want them to act as the leafy component of the salad and their freshness should offset the earthiness of the rice. If you can't find harissa paste, feel free to add a minced clove of fresh garlic and some freshly chopped red chili pepper in its place.

If you want to make this ahead of time, cook the rice and dress it up to a day ahead. Leave off the cranberries, herbs, nuts and cheese until just before serving. Leftovers will keep for up to 3 days in the fridge, although the nuts will soften over time.

Brussels Sprouts and Couscous Salad

SERVES
8 as part of a banquet

PREP TIME
20 min

COOKING TIME
15 min

OVEN SETTINGS
212°F/100°C
Steam
100% Humidity

INGREDIENTS

Dressing

1/2 cup (125ml) extra virgin olive oil
1/4 cup (60ml) water
2 Tbs apple cider vinegar
1 shallot, finely diced
2 Tbsp Dijon mustard
Salt and pepper, to taste

Salad

1 cup (160g) pearl couscous
1 1/2 cups (375ml) light vegetable stock
1lb (450g) brussels sprouts, divided equally into two bowls
2 Tbsp extra virgin olive oil
1/2 cup (65g) pecans, toasted, roughly chopped
1/2 cup (50g) dried cranberries (or currants)
Salt and pepper to taste

This accidentally vegan salad is packed with shaved and roasted Brussels sprouts, pearl couscous, cranberries and toasted pecans. It's a more modern way to add the traditional Brussels sprout to your Christmas table. The salad is hearty, delicious, and deserves a place on your menu whether you have vegan diners or not.

I prefer to make and serve this within a couple of hours, because I find the Brussels sprouts taste a little muddy if they sit around too long.

METHOD

1. Make the dressing. Put all the ingredients into a lidded jar and shake well to combine. Set aside.
2. Preheat your oven to 212°F/100°C, Steam, 100% humidity. Put the couscous into a shallow pan and cover with the stock. Put into the preheated oven and cook for 15 minutes. When the couscous is done, remove from the oven, fluff with a fork and put it into a serving bowl.
3. Change the oven settings to 450°F/220°C, Combination Steam, 80% humidity.
4. Trim and halve one portion of the Brussels sprouts and put into a roasting pan. Drizzle with oil and cook until they're tender and starting to blacken at the edges, about 12 minutes.
5. Thinly slice the other portion of the Brussels sprouts and add to the serving bowl with the couscous (yes, these sprouts are raw; they're meant to be!).
6. When the roasted sprouts are done, put them into the bowl with the couscous and raw shredded sprouts. Add the pecans, cranberries and a little salt and pepper.
7. Drizzle dressing on top and toss to coat. Taste and adjust if necessary, adding more salt or pepper to the salad.
8. Serve immediately, warm, or allow to cool to room temperature.

Bacon Wrapped Sausages

MAKES
12 sausages

PREP TIME
10 min

COOKING TIME
20 min

OVEN SETTINGS
350°F/180°C
Combination Steam
30% Humidity

INGREDIENTS

12 raw sausages, mini/small size (use cocktail sausages, little smokies or wieners instead if preferred; see note for cooking times)

6 slices streaky bacon, halved lengthwise

1/2 cup firmly packed (90g) brown sugar

1/4 tsp cayenne pepper (optional)

1/4 tsp ground black pepper

METHOD

1. Preheat your oven to 350°F/180°C, Combination Steam, 30% humidity. Grease a baking sheet and set aside.
2. Wrap each sausage in one of the cut pieces of bacon and secure with a toothpick.
3. Mix the sugar, cayenne and black pepper in a shallow bowl and add the sausages, turning to coat.
4. Spread the sugar-coated sausages onto the prepared pan. If you find the sugar mixture hasn't stuck very well (this will depend on how dry your bacon is), sprinkle a little over the sausages once they're in the pan.
5. Cook until the bacon is crispy and golden, about 20 minutes, turning after 10 minutes and then again after 15 to coat in the sugar and bacon fat which collects on the bottom of the pan. If you'd like a little extra color, broil/grill the sausages briefly to finish.
6. Serve hot or warm. If pre-cooking to reheat later, chill immediately and store in an airtight container for up to 2 days. Reheat using the same settings that you cooked at, for around 10 minutes.

Bacon wrapped sausages are a versatile appetizer or breakfast dish. They're very simple to make and incredibly popular with kids and adults alike.

The timings below are given for raw sausages. You can use cooked smoked sausages, wieners or similar, just drop the cooking time by around 5 minutes.

Scale this recipe up or down as much as you like – the cooking time will remain the same as long as you cook the sausages in a single layer with a little room in the pan.

Sour Cherry and Pecan Stuffing

SERVES
10 as part of a banquet

PREP TIME
20 min

COOKING TIME
25 min

OVEN SETTINGS
350°F/180°C
Combination Steam
50% Humidity

INGREDIENTS

1lb (450g) stale bread, cut into 1 inch (2.5cm) pieces

1 Tbsp extra virgin olive oil

1lb (450g) fresh pork sausages, casings removed

5 Tbsp (85g) unsalted butter, cubed

1 large onion, finely chopped

2 stalks celery, finely chopped

3 cloves garlic, minced

3 sprigs parsley, finely chopped (include the stalks)

3 sprigs thyme, leaves picked and chopped

1/2 tsp ground black pepper

2 cups (500ml) chicken or turkey stock

1 egg, lightly beaten

2/3 cup (100g) dried sour cherries, coarsely chopped (dried cranberries make a good substitute)

2/3 cup (85g) pecan nuts, coarsely chopped

You'll never stuff a bird again once you discover how good pan-baked stuffing is. Cooked using combi steam, this sausage meat mix with juicy sour cherries and crunchy pecans becomes crispy on top and soft, salty and fragrant underneath. It's so good I could just about skip the turkey altogether.

The ingredients in this recipe are very adaptable. Change up the flavors and texture by choosing different types of sausages or bread, and swapping the herbs, dried fruit and nuts for others that take your fancy.

You can fully assemble the stuffing ahead of time, cover and refrigerate for up to 2 days, or freeze up to 4 weeks. If freezing, thaw overnight in the fridge before cooking. Bake just before serving for the best texture.

METHOD

1. Preheat your oven to 350°F/180°C (no steam). Grease a 9x13 inch (23x33cm) rectangular baking dish and set aside. Have a second large baking pan ready (no need to grease this one).
2. Put the cubed bread in a single layer on the second pan and cook until toasted but not too browned, about eight minutes. Remove from the oven and transfer to a large bowl. Leave the oven at the same temperature but change the setting to Combination Steam, 50% humidity.
3. Heat the oil in a frypan over medium heat. Cook the sausage meat until browned all over, breaking it up as it cooks.
4. Add the butter, onions, celery, garlic, herbs and pepper to the meat. Cook until the vegetables are softened, about five minutes.
5. Tip the meat mixture into the bowl with the bread, then pour in the stock, whisked egg, sour cherries and nuts. Mix everything together well until all the liquid has been absorbed by the bread.
6. Put the stuffing into the prepared baking dish, spreading it evenly to the edges. Cook until it's golden brown all over, about 25 minutes. Serve hot or warm.

Dessert

By the time dessert comes around after a big Christmas meal, I am usually exhausted enough that I don't want to do any more hard work! These are the desserts I turn to, because every one of them can be completely made ahead of time. The most you'll have to do before serving is warm a pudding in your steam oven.

My favorite thing about Christmas dessert? Whatever isn't eaten makes for very indulgent leftovers in the quieter post-Christmas days to follow.

Crème Caramel

Chocolate Pots de Creme

Chocolate and Raspberry Roulade

Fig, Apricot and Orange Christmas Pudding

Individual Steamed Christmas Puddings

Christmas Cheesecake

Basque Burnt Cheesecake

Mint Chocolate Cheesecake

Crème Caramel

			 OVEN SETTINGS
MAKES 6	PREP TIME 20 min	COOKING TIME 1 hour 30 min	175°F/80°C Steam 100% Humidity

INGREDIENTS

For the custard

1 cup (250ml) whole milk

1 cup (250ml) cream (whipping or pouring)

1 vanilla bean (or 1 tsp vanilla extract)

1/2 cup (100g) superfine (caster) sugar

2 eggs

4 egg yolks

For the caramel

2/3 cup (130g) superfine (caster) sugar

Silky soft crème caramel is the ultimate make-ahead impressive dessert! Cook these in your steam oven to get perfectly set texture and avoid the need for a water bath.

Start this recipe the day before. Cooked crème caramels will keep, covered, in the fridge for up to 4 days. I do not recommend freezing them as the custard can split when thawed.

METHOD

1. Grease 6 x 4oz (1/2 cup) ramekins or jars with butter. Put them all into a baking dish and set aside. Preheat your oven to 175°F/80°C, Steam, 100% humidity.
2. Pour the milk and cream into a small pan. Scrape the seeds from the vanilla pod, and add the seeds and pod to the pan. Bring to a simmer over medium heat, then turn off the heat, cover and leave to infuse while you make the caramel.
3. Put the sugar for the caramel into a deep saucepan and just barely cover it with water. Bring to a simmer over medium heat, then cook until it's syrupy and turning a golden amber color. Quickly remove from heat and divide the caramel between the ramekins or jars. Swirl to evenly cover the bases and come a little way up the sides. Set aside.
4. When the infused milk has cooled to lukewarm, remove the vanilla pod. Add the sugar and whisk to combine. Tip in the eggs and yolks and whisk thoroughly, then pour the mixture through a sieve into a jug. Leave the mixture to settle for 15 minutes, then skim any foam from the top of the bowl.
5. Pour the custard into the caramel-coated jars, dividing it evenly.
6. Cook the crèmes for 1 hour, then remove from the oven. Cool to room temperature on the bench, then refrigerate overnight. The crèmes need this overnight chilling and setting time so the caramel can soften into a liquid sauce.
7. To unmold, run a slim knife around the inside of each jar and invert onto plates, letting the liquid caramel run over the custard.

Chocolate Pots de Creme

MAKES
8

PREP TIME
20 min

COOKING TIME
1 1/2 hours

OVEN SETTINGS
165°F/75°C
Steam
100% Humidity

INGREDIENTS

2 1/2 cups (625ml) pouring or whipping cream

1 tsp vanilla bean paste or extract

5oz (150g) bittersweet chocolate, chopped (I prefer 85% cocoa solids)

6 egg yolks

1/3 cup (75g) superfine (caster) sugar

METHOD

1. Heat the cream and vanilla in a saucepan over medium heat until it comes to the boil. Remove from heat and tip in the chocolate. Give it a stir until the chocolate melts and the mixture is smooth.
2. Whisk the egg yolks and sugar in a large bowl until well combined. Gradually whisk in the hot chocolate mixture. Strain through a fine sieve into a jug and carefully skim off any remaining foam from the top.
3. Set out your ramekins or jars in a baking dish and pour the mixture evenly between them. Cover each one with aluminum foil or jar lids.
4. Set oven to 165°F/75°C, Steam, 100% humidity. Place the baking dish in the oven and cook for 1 1/2 hours. The cremes should be gently set. Allow to cool to room temperature, then refrigerate for at least 4 hours and up to 3 days. Serve cold with clotted or whipped cream.

These are rich and creamy without being too sweet. Perhaps my favorite thing about them, though, is that you can completely prepare them up to 3 days ahead of time. All you need to do on the day is pull them out of the fridge and top with a spoonful of cream.

For a bit of fun, try a pots de creme buffet, setting them out with an array of toppings for everyone to help themselves. I like fresh raspberries, crushed shortbread cookies, tiny meringues and little sugar or chocolate pearls.

You'll need 8 x 1/2 cup (125ml) ramekins or small glass jars for this recipe.

Chocolate and Raspberry Roulade

SERVES
8

PREP TIME
40 min

COOKING TIME
12 min

OVEN SETTINGS
350°F/180°C
Combination Steam
50% Humidity

INGREDIENTS

For the sponge cake
5 eggs
1/2 cup (100g) superfine (caster) sugar
1/2 cup (60g) all-purpose (plain) flour
1/3 cup (40g) cocoa powder (I use Dutch processed)
1 tsp vanilla extract
For the ganache and filling
2 1/2 cups (625ml) heavy/pouring cream
14oz (400g) bittersweet/dark chocolate, chopped
1 Tbsp unsalted butter
4oz (125g) fresh raspberries, plus extra berries to decorate

METHOD

1. Preheat your oven to 350F/180C, Combination Steam, 50% humidity. Line a 9x13 inch (23x33cm) pan with parchment paper and set aside.
2. Beat the eggs and sugar in a stand mixer or with an electric whisk until thick and pale, about 5-6 minutes.
3. Sift the flour and cocoa over the egg mixture, add the vanilla and fold together very carefully with a metal spoon. The idea is to gently incorporate the dry ingredients into the eggs without losing all the volume you've just whipped into them.
4. Gently spread the batter into the lined pan and bake until it's slightly puffed and set through, about 10 minutes. Don't overbake or it'll be difficult to roll.
5. Turn the hot cake immediately onto a clean kitchen towel. Gently peel the paper away and, as soon as the cake is cool enough to handle, roll it up from the long side, rolling the towel inside it as you go (this stops it sticking to itself later). Leave rolled up to cool while you make the ganache.

This pretty rolled sponge cake is deceptively easy to make, but you will need a stand mixer or electric whisk. Beating the eggs and sugar for the sponge, and then the ganache for the filling takes enough effort that I wouldn't want to do it by hand.

The one thing to watch for in this recipe is when it comes to the final ganache step, where you mix extra cream through the whipped ganache to make the filling. Depending on the water content of your cream, it's possible for the mixture to split. If it does, don't panic! Have some very soft butter on hand and with your mixer running on low speed, add in a teaspoon or two of the butter at a time, fully incorporating it each time and watching for the magical moment when everything comes back together into a fluffy mass. It might take several spoonfuls of butter and a lot of mixing, but this fix won't affect the end taste except to make your filling a little more creamy.

METHOD Continued...

6. Heat 1 3/4 cups of the cream in a medium saucepan until it just comes to boiling point, then remove from heat and add the chocolate and butter. Leave for five minutes to let chocolate melt, then stir until smooth. Set aside to cool for until it's lukewarm.
7. Put the cooled chocolate mixture into the bowl of a stand mixer and whip until light, anywhere from 7 to 15 minutes. Transfer two thirds of the mixture into another bowl and set aside, then add the remaining cream to the remaining ganache and mix in on low speed (if it happens to split, follow the directions in the headnote to fix).
8. Unroll the cake and spread it with the lighter, extra-cream ganache. Halve the raspberries and scatter over the ganache, then re-roll.
9. Spread the remaining darker ganache over the roll to cover it, making swirled decorative patterns. Decorate with additional raspberries and dust with powdered sugar if you like.
10. This cake can be made and fully assembled up to 8 hours before serving. It is actually easier to slice neatly if it's made at least a couple of hours ahead. Store it in the fridge until 30 minutes before you want to serve. Serve in slices with extra berries on the side.

Fig, Apricot and Orange Christmas Pudding

MAKES
1 quart (1 litre) pudding, to serve 8-10

PREP TIME
20 min plus overnight macerating time

COOKING TIME
6 hours
Reheating Time
1 1/2 hours

OVEN SETTINGS
212°F/100°C
Steam
100% Humidity

INGREDIENTS

1 cup (125g) soft dried figs, chopped

1 cup (150g) glace/candied apricots, chopped

1 cup (125g) pitted soft prunes, chopped

1 cup (125g) raisins or sultanas

1 cup (125g) dried cranberries

1/4 cup (60ml) brandy, Cointreau or dry sherry

Zest and juice of 2 oranges

1 cup, lightly packed (75g) fresh white breadcrumbs

1/2 cup (75g) all-purpose (plain) flour

1 tsp ground cinnamon

1 tsp ground ginger

1/2 tsp ground nutmeg

1/4 tsp ground cloves

1/2 cup (60g) chopped macadamia nuts

1 cup, firmly packed (200g) dark brown sugar

3 1/2 oz (100g) unsalted butter, softened

2 eggs, lightly beaten

Christmas pudding improves with age, though I've made this one as late as the week before Christmas and it was still excellent. It stores well in the fridge for up to 6 weeks, after which I'd recommend putting it in the freezer to store. Thaw in the fridge for a couple of days before you plan to heat and serve.

If you prefer individual puddings you can cook this in half-cup pudding molds. They'll take 1 1/2 hours to cook and about half an hour to reheat in the steam oven.

When you chop the dried fruits, aim for pieces around the size of a raisin.

I serve Christmas pudding with vanilla ice cream, but a good custard is welcome too.

METHOD

1. Put the dried fruit into a large bowl with the alcohol, orange zest and juice. Set aside overnight to macerate.
2. Grease a 1 quart (1 litre) ceramic or metal pudding bowl and line the base with a small circle of parchment paper.
3. Add the remaining ingredients to the bowl of fruit and stir until very well combined.
4. Firmly pack the mixture into the pudding bowl. Lay a piece of aluminum foil large enough to cover the bowl over a piece of parchment or baking paper, and fold a pleat into the center of both pieces. Use this to tightly cover the bowl (paper side underneath).
5. Put the covered pudding into your steam oven and set to 212°F/100°C, Steam, 100% humidity. Cook for 6 hours. If your oven is not plumbed you'll likely need to top up the water tank at least once during this time.
6. When the pudding is cooked, remove from the oven and let it cool for an hour or two on the counter. Transfer to the fridge to mature for at least a couple of days or up to several weeks.
7. When it's time to serve the pudding, repeat the steaming process for 1 1/2 hours to heat through. Serve hot with ice cream or custard.

Individual Steamed Christmas Puddings

MAKES
12 puddings

PREP TIME
30 min plus 1 day soaking time

COOKING TIME
1 hr 30 min

OVEN SETTINGS
212°F/100°C
Steam
100% Humidity

INGREDIENTS

1.75 lb (800g) mixed dried fruit, chopped into pea-sized pieces

4 oz (125g) almonds, chopped

1/4 cup (60ml) brandy

1 cup (250g) unsalted butter, softened

1 1/4 cups, firmly packed (220g) brown sugar

1 orange, zested and juiced

4 eggs

1 cup (130g) all-purpose (plain) flour

1 tsp ground ginger

1/2 tsp ground cinnamon

1/4 tsp ground cloves

1/4 tsp ground nutmeg

2 cups lightly packed (125g) fresh white breadcrumbs

Steamed Christmas puddings are a British classic. These small versions have the same traditional ingredients and taste but they cook much faster. They make a pretty dessert or a lovely food gift when wrapped in clear bags with a ribbon around the top.

Use a combination of your choice when it comes to dried fruit. I like to make sure it's at least half vine fruits (raisins, sultanas and currants), but I always add a little candied ginger because I love it, as well as some candied orange slices. Some stores sell pre-packaged mixed dried fruit; I really dislike it. The pre-packaged stuff generally contains candied peel with artificial citrus essence added, which smells and tastes awful.

You'll need to soak the mixed fruit and nuts overnight before making your puddings. Ideally, puddings should be cooked and then matured in the fridge for a few weeks, but they'll be good to eat anywhere from just a few days after cooking. If you'd like to store them for up to a few months, freeze the puddings until the day of serving. Reheat from frozen at 212°F/100°C, Steam, 100% humidity for 45 minutes.

If you have half-cup individual pudding molds, use these for your Christmas puddings. Otherwise a standard sized 12-cup muffin pan will work fine.

METHOD

1. A day before you want to cook the puddings, put the fruit and almonds into a bowl and pour the brandy over the top. Mix to coat everything with the alcohol, then cover and leave overnight.
2. The next day, grease 12 individual half-cup pudding molds or a 12-cup standard muffin pan. Line the base of each mold with a small piece of parchment paper and set aside.
3. Cream the butter, sugar, orange rind and juice until light and fluffy. Add the eggs, one at a time, beating to incorporate each one before adding the next. If the mixture curdles when the last couple of eggs are added, don't worry.
4. Add the flour and spices to the butter mixture and mix just to combine, then add the breadcrumbs and soaked fruit and mix until well combined.
5. Divide the mixture evenly into the prepared pans, then cover the puddings with parchment paper to fit (you'll need a single large piece of paper for a muffin pan, or small single pieces for individual molds).
6. Put the puddings into your steam oven and set to 212°F/100°C, Steam, 100% humidity. Cook for 1 1/2 hours, then remove and cool puddings before turning out of the pan.
7. Store the puddings, wrapped in wax paper inside an airtight container, in the fridge for up to 3 weeks. Brush with extra brandy every few days during this time. Serve with custard.

A Trio Of Cheesecakes

Somehow, cheesecake has become a Christmas staple around here. It's not really traditional, but my family loves them so much that there's always at least one on the table for dessert. It's a trend I'm happy to embrace because they're easy to make ahead of time, and the perfect indulgent end to a special meal.

Christmas Cheesecake

SERVES
12

PREP TIME
30 min

COOKING TIME
2 hours plus overnight chilling time

OVEN SETTINGS
175°F/80°C
Steam
100% Humidity

INGREDIENTS

For the crust:
1lb (450g) ginger snap or ginger nut cookies
1/2 cup (125g) unsalted butter, melted

For the filling:
32oz (1kg) cream cheese (full fat, brick style), softened
1 1/4 cups (225g) granulated sugar
5 eggs
2 tsp vanilla bean paste or extract

For the topping:
1lb (450g) pitted cherries (frozen is fine)
Juice of 1 large lemon
1/4 cup (60g) (1/4 cup) granulated sugar
2 Tbsp cornstarch (cornflour)

Christmas in Australia falls at the peak of cherry season, and we always have a large bowl of fresh cherries on the table for people to grab throughout the day. I love cherries atop a silky, rich cheesecake too, especially when that's combined with a gingery crumb crust.

If you're not celebrating Christmas during your cherry season, frozen pitted cherries are a very fine substitute for the topping.

You'll need a 9 inch (22cm) springform pan to cook this cheesecake, and you need to start the recipe a day ahead.

METHOD

1. 1.Preheat your oven to 175°F/80°C, Steam, 100% humidity. Line the base of a 9 inch (22cm) springform pan with parchment paper, sealing the collar of the pan around the paper and leaving an overhang sticking out at the sides.
2. Make the crust. Grind the ginger snaps in a food processor until they resemble fine breadcrumbs. With the motor running, pour in the melted butter and process until mixed. Press the crumbs into the bottom and up the sides of the prepared pan, compacting as much as possible. Use the base of a glass to smooth and compact the crust, pressing it into the corners so it's even. Put the pan in the freezer for 20 minutes while you make the filling.
3. Make the filling. Rinse and dry your food processor bowl. Put the cream cheese and sugar into the processor and run until well mixed and smooth. Add the eggs and vanilla and run the processor again, just until the mixture is smooth. Don't overmix or your cheesecake will end up with air bubbles in it.
4. Pour the filling into the chilled crust and tap the pan lightly on the counter to remove excess air. Cover the top of the pan with aluminum foil, then place in the oven and cook for two hours.
5. At the end of the cooking time, the cheesecake should be set but with a wobble in the center. Let it cool in the switched-off oven for an hour, then carefully remove the foil so you don't get condensation on top of your cake. Refrigerate overnight or up to three days.
6. When you're ready to serve, carefully run a thin-bladed knife around the edge of the cake to loosen, then remove the collar from the pan and transfer the cheesecake to a serving plate. Spoon over the cherry topping and cut into thin slices with a hot knife to serve.
7. To make the cherry topping: put all the topping ingredients in a saucepan and bring to the boil, stirring occasionally. Reduce heat to a simmer and cook gently for a few minutes until the juices have thickened. Allow to cool to room temperature.

Basque Burnt Cheesecake

SERVES
12

PREP TIME
15 min

COOKING TIME
55 min plus overnight chilling

OVEN SETTINGS
400°F/200°C
Combination Steam
30% Humidity

INGREDIENTS

32oz (1kg) cream cheese (full fat, brick style), at room temperature

1 1/4 cups (250g) granulated sugar

6 eggs

2 cups (500ml) heavy cream

1/2 tsp fine salt

1 vanilla bean, split and seeds scraped or 1 1/2 tsp vanilla extract

1/4 cup (35g) all-purpose (plain) flour

This cheesecake is intentionally cooked at a high temperature to create a burnished, toasty top which complements the creamy interior perfectly. It's really easy to put together because there's no crust.

Serve this, unadorned, at a cool room temperature rather than straight from the fridge. The cheesecake will keep, chilled and covered, for up to 5 days. It can be frozen, well wrapped, for up to 2 months. Thaw overnight in the fridge before serving.

You'll need a 9 inch (22cm) springform pan for this recipe, and you should start it at least a day ahead of time.

METHOD

1. Preheat your oven to 400°F/200°C, Combination Steam, 30% humidity.
2. Use two layers of parchment paper to line a 9 inch (22cm) springform pan, overlapping the two layers and scrunching them into the pan and up the sides. I do this by scrunching the paper into a ball and then flattening it out again so it's more flexible. You don't need to get the paper smooth, it should be what I like to call 'intentionally rustic'.
3. Put the cream cheese and sugar into a stand mixer with the paddle attachment fitted. Mix on medium speed until well combined and smooth, scraping down the sides as necessary.
4. Add the eggs, one at a time, with the mixer running. Mix each one in completely before adding the next.
5. Add the remaining ingredients and mix on low speed until completely combined. Don't mix longer than necessary as you don't want to aerate the mixture too much.
6. Pour the batter into the prepared pan and place into the preheated oven. Cook until the cheesecake is dark brown on top, puffy and very wobbly, approximately 55 minutes.
7. Cool the cheesecake to lukewarm on the counter. It will sink significantly in the center as it cools, this is normal.
8. Refrigerate the cheesecake for at least eight hours or overnight to set.
9. To serve, allow the cake to come to a cool room temperature and then slice with a hot knife, cleaning the blade between each cut to get nice clean slices.

Mint Chocolate Cheesecake

SERVES
12

PREP TIME
25 min

COOKING TIME
2 hours plus overnight chilling time

OVEN SETTINGS
175°F/80°C
Steam
100% Humidity

INGREDIENTS

For the crust
30 Oreo cookies
1/4 cup (60g) unsalted butter, melted

For the filling
32oz (1kg) cream cheese (full fat, brick style), softened
1 cup (200g) granulated sugar
8oz (220g) white chocolate, melted and cooled (1 1/2 cups chips)
1 1/2 tsp peppermint extract
4 eggs
2-3 drops green food coloring (optional)

For the topping
6 oz (175g) bittersweet chocolate, chopped (or 1 cup chips)
3/4 cup (185ml) heavy cream
2 Peppermint Crisp candy bars (2 x 35 g) roughly chopped, or other peppermint chocolate candies, chopped

Mint chocolate cheesecake is rich, indulgent and creamy, with a hit of peppermint to brighten things up! It's a beautiful special occasion cake. The color comes from a touch of green food coloring, which is optional but does add to the minty vibes.

I use Peppermint Crisp bars to decorate my cheesecake; they're widely available in Australia but if you can't find them, another chocolate mint candy will work just fine. Try Andes mints in the USA or After Eights in the UK.

You'll need a 9 inch (22cm) springform pan to cook this cheesecake, and you need to start the recipe a day ahead.

METHOD

1. 1.Make the crust. Preheat your oven to 175°F/80°C, Steam, 100% humidity. Line the base of a 9 inch (22cm) springform pan with parchment paper, sealing the collar of the pan around the paper and leaving an overhang sticking out at the sides.
2. Put the Oreos in a food processor and pulse until they form crumbs. Pour in melted butter and mix using the food processor. Press the crumbs into the bottom and up the sides of the prepared pan, compacting as much as possible. You can use the base of a glass to smooth and compact the crust, pressing it into the corners so it's more even. Put the pan in the freezer for 20 minutes while you make the filling.
3. Make the filling. Rinse and dry your food processor bowl. Put the cream cheese and sugar into the processor and run until well mixed and smooth. Add the remaining filling ingredients. Run the processor again, just until the mixture is smooth. Don't overmix or your cheesecake will end up with air bubbles in it.
4. Pour the filling into the chilled crust and tap the pan lightly on the counter to remove excess air. Cover the top of the pan with aluminum foil, then place in the oven and cook for two hours.
5. At the end of the cooking time, the cheesecake should be set but with a wobble in the center. Let it cool in the switched-off oven for an hour, then carefully remove the foil so you don't get condensation on top of your cake. Refrigerate overnight or up to three days.

METHOD Continued...

6. When you're ready to serve, carefully run a thin-bladed knife around the edge of the cake to loosen, then remove the collar from the pan and transfer the cheesecake to a serving plate. Spread or drizzle the ganache over the cake and top with chopped peppermint candy.
7. To make ganache topping: put the chocolate into a bowl and set aside. In a small saucepan, bring cream just to a boil. Pour the hot cream over the chocolate. Let it sit for a couple of minutes, then stir with a whisk until smooth. Allow to cool to room temperature before spreading it onto the cake.
8. To serve, cut slices from the cold cake with a knife dipped briefly into hot water and dried off after each cut (this makes for cleanly cut slices).
9. Leftover cheesecake will keep, refrigerated, for up to five days.

Gifting

I'm aware most of you come to this book for steam oven dishes, and I'm thrilled about that! But I wanted to include this chapter of mostly non-steam-oven recipes too. Food gifts around Christmas time are a huge part of the joy of the season, and I wouldn't be giving you a fully fledged collection of recipes without sharing the gifts I bake year in and year out – steam oven or not!

Make one or two of these gifts, or work through the entire chapter and package up the most delightful gift boxes for friends, family and neighbors through December.

Sweet and Spicy Party Nuts

Spiced Fruit Mince Pies

Panforte with Ginger, Apricots and Macadamias

Traditional Shortbread

Best Ever Chocolate Gingerbread Cookies

Burnt Caramel Truffles

Sweet and Spicy Party Nuts

SERVES
10 as a snack

PREP TIME
10 min

COOKING TIME
18 min

OVEN SETTINGS
350°F/180°C
Convection
No Steam

INGREDIENTS

1 Tbsp salted butter
1/2 cup (100g) granulated sugar
1/4 cup (60ml) water
2 cups (300g) whole raw almonds
2 cups (260g) whole raw cashew nuts
1 1/4 tsp flaky salt
1/2 tsp black pepper
1/2 tsp ground cumin
1/4 tsp cayenne pepper

METHOD

1. Preheat your oven to 350°F/180°C, Convection/Fan Forced (no steam). Line a baking sheet with parchment paper and set aside. Put the nuts into a mixing bowl and set aside.
2. Put the butter, sugar and water into a small pan and cook over medium heat until the sugar is dissolved and the mixture comes to a simmer. Remove from heat.
3. Stir the salt, pepper and spices into the syrup and pour over the nuts. Stir to combine so all the nuts are coated in the syrup, then spread the nuts and any excess syrup onto the prepared baking sheet.
4. Bake for 10 minutes, then stir to make sure all the nuts are separate and evenly coated. Return to the oven for a further five minutes then stir again. At this point, if the nuts are nicely toasted and the coating is just slightly sticky, they're done. If they aren't toasted enough, give them a few minutes extra in the oven. Remove from the oven and stir a couple of times as the nuts cool so they remain separate. They will harden on cooling.
5. Store the nuts in a well sealed container in a cool, dry place for up to a few weeks.

These nuts are a little sweet, a little salty and just spicy enough to give them a kick. They're great as a canape with drinks and make an easy last-minute homemade gift.

You can change up the nuts to use almost any other type, so long as you stick to the same total volume. Pecans, macadamias or peanuts are great additions. I steer clear of walnuts as they tend to toast and burn faster than the sugar and spice coating can cook.

The nuts keep for up to a couple of weeks in an airtight container or tightly lidded jar. If you're gifting them, they'll keep best in tightly sealed clear plastic gift bags.

Spiced Fruit Mince Pies

MAKES
about 4 dozen

PREP TIME
1 hour

COOKING TIME
12 min

OVEN SETTINGS
375°F/190°C
Combination Steam
30% Humidity

INGREDIENTS

1 1/2 cups (150g) shelled walnuts
3 1/2 cups (475g) all-purpose (plain) flour
1 1/2 tsp ground cinnamon
1/2 tsp ground ginger
1/2 tsp ground nutmeg
1/4 tsp ground cloves
1/4 tsp fine salt
1 1/4 cups (165g) confectioners (icing) sugar
1 1/4 cups (285g) unsalted butter, chilled and diced
1 egg yolk
Zest of 1 lemon
1-2 Tbsp ice cold water
2 x 14.5 oz (2 x 410g) jars bought fruit mincemeat, or equivalent home-made
Extra confectioners (icing) sugar, for dusting

METHOD

1. Make the pastry. Put walnuts into the bowl of a food processor and process until they are finely ground but not a paste. Add the rest of the dry ingredients and pulse to combine. Add the butter and pulse again until the mixture resembles breadcrumbs, then drop in the egg yolk and lemon zest. Run the machine until the dough just comes together in a mass. What you're looking for is a dough which is soft but not too sticky – it shouldn't stick to your fingers when you pinch a piece off to check it.
2. Split the dough in half and turn out onto 2 large pieces of cling film. Pat each piece into a disc about an inch (2.5cm) thick, then wrap and refrigerate for at least 30 minutes or up to 24 hours.
3. When you're ready to make the pies, preheat your oven to 375°F/190°C, Combination Steam, 30% humidity. Lightly grease 2 x 12-cup patty pan trays.

This recipe makes a lot of pies. You could halve it but I always find a full batch seems to disappear almost overnight, between hungry festive guests and packing some up for gifting.

You'll need a food processor to make the walnut pastry. It's a very short pastry and can be difficult to work with in warm climates, but I think it's worth it. If you find yours is a bit soft to handle after rolling out, just return it to the fridge for 10-15 minutes then try again. I've been known to do that two or three times over the course of a couple of hours, in between other household tasks.

Some years I make fruit mince (mincemeat) for these pies, but frequently I buy it ready-made. Robertsons is the most commonly available brand and can be bought online in most countries. The quantity below is approximate, I generally get through 1 1/2 jars but it depends how large your pans are and how full you want to make the pies.

The baking trays I use for my pies are what's commonly referred to as patty pan trays. They're non-stick with rounded bases, and readily available online if you don't have any.

The pies will keep in a container at room temperature for two or three days before the pastry starts to soften. They store well in the freezer for about 6 weeks, and just need an hour on the kitchen bench to thaw.

METHOD Continued...

4. Using a little flour to dust your counter and rolling pin, roll one piece of the pastry out to approximately 1/8 inch (3mm) thick. Using a round cutter a little larger than the cups in your patty pan, cut 24 circles and gently lay them into the pan, pressing to the bottom. If any cracks appear in the pastry just press it back together gently, it should seal up fine while cooking.
5. Roll any offcuts back together on a piece of parchment paper and cut decorative tops for the pies.
6. Put about a teaspoon of fruit mince into each pastry case, then top with your cut shapes. Bake the pies until the pastry is golden and mince bubbling, about 12 minutes. Remove from the oven and leave to cool before carefully removing the pies and repeating the process with the other half of the chilled pastry.
7. Serve pies at room temperature, dusted with confectioners sugar.

Panforte with Ginger, Apricots and Macadamias

| MAKES
one 9 inch (22cm) round or
one 8 inch (20cm) square cake | PREP TIME
15 min | COOKING TIME
45 min | OVEN SETTINGS
300°F/150°C
Convection
No Steam |

INGREDIENTS

10 1/2 oz (300g) good quality white chocolate chopped

3/4 cup (265g) clear honey

1 1/4 cups (185g) all-purpose (plain) flour

1 tsp ground ginger

1 tsp ground allspice

1/2 tsp ground cinnamon

1/4 tsp white pepper

2oz (60g) stem ginger, chopped (around 1/3 cup chopped volume)

2 oz (55g) candied orange slices, chopped (around 1/4 cup chopped volume)

2 oz (55g) candied apricots or peaches, chopped (around 1/3 cup chopped volume

3/4 cup (100g) macadamia nuts, halved (3.5oz)

3/4 cup (100g) blanched almonds (3.5oz)

Confectioners (icing) sugar, for dusting

METHOD

1. Preheat your oven to 300°F,/150°C, Convection/Fan Forced (no steam). Grease a 9 inch (22cm) round or 8 inch (20cm) square cake pan and line the base with parchment paper.
2. Put the white chocolate and honey in a pan over very low heat, stirring often, until the chocolate is melted and the mixture smooth. If your stove doesn't go down to a very gentle low heat I'd recommend doing this step using a double boiler so you don't burn the chocolate.
3. Combine the flour and spices in a bowl and whisk to combine. Add the fruits and nuts and give everything a stir to coat them in the flour.
4. Add the chocolate/honey mixture to the bowl and stir well. I find clean hands easiest for this as the mixture is very stiff. Make sure everything is evenly mixed and there are no lumps of flour remaining.

This flat, Italian-style confection, also known as Siena cake, makes a wonderful alternative to a traditional Christmas fruit cake. It's denser and richer, packed with spices, nuts and candied fruit. It also keeps exceptionally well, improving with age, and is sturdy enough to pack and ship easily.

You'll see I've simply noted 'chopped' for the glace/candied fruits, without giving a guide to what sized pieces. It's up to you – finely chopped fruit will give a finer texture, roughly chopped makes for a chunkier panforte. I like to chop the ginger and orange into roughly quarter inch (1/2 cm) pieces so they distribute evenly through the batter, but I make the apricots about twice that size for a bit of textural interest.

Take care not to overcook your panforte. The cake should be lightly golden all over but still quite soft to touch when it comes out of the oven. It will firm up as it cools, and even if you've been a bit cautious and under-baked it, it'll just be a little more fudgy than normal. I promise no one will notice.

Panforte will keep, well wrapped in a cool, dark place, for months. Serve it in thin slices with strong coffee for morning tea or a liqueur after dinner.

METHOD Continued...

5. Scrape the mixture into the prepared pan and press out gently with your hands or the back of a spoon until it's even. Bake until golden but soft, about 45 minutes. Let it cool slightly, then run a thin knife around the edge of the pan to loosen the sides.
6. Cool the panforte completely in the pan, then turn it out and wrap well in aluminum foil for storage. Keep in a cool dark place and when you're ready to serve, dust it with confectioners (icing) sugar and cut into thin wedges.

Traditional Shortbread

MAKES
approximately 24 cookies

PREP TIME
20 min

COOKING TIME
30 min

OVEN SETTINGS
350°F/150°C
Convection
No steam

INGREDIENTS

1 cup (250g) unsalted butter, room temperature
1/2 cup (100g) superfine (caster) sugar
½ teaspoon fine salt
1 3/4 cups (300g) all-purpose (plain) flour, sifted
1/2 cup (90g) fine rice flour

My traditional shortbread recipe relies on just a handful of ingredients to make a sandy, buttery, perfectly textured cookie. Don't be underwhelmed by their simplicity, though. These are hands down my favorite cookies to eat during the holidays.

Rice flour gives these cookies their characteristic sandy, slightly gritty texture. You could make shortbread just using wheat flour, but it'll be softer and smoother.

This dough can be cut into shapes using cutters or cookie stamps, or made into traditional wedges by creating a hand-formed circle that gets cut into pieces after baking.

Shortbread will keep for a couple of weeks in an airtight container at room temperature, or can be frozen, well wrapped, for up to six months.

METHOD

1. Preheat your oven to 300°F/150°C, Conventional/Top and Bottom elements (no steam). Line a couple of cookie sheets with parchment paper and set aside.
2. Put the butter, sugar and salt into the bowl of a stand mixer fitted with the paddle attachment and beat on medium speed until creamy. The time this takes will vary depending on how soft your butter is to begin with, and how strong your mixer is. You aren't going for very fluffy butter here, though. Just mix to the point where the color has lightened and the texture is nice and soft.
3. While the butter and sugar are creaming, put the flour and rice flour into a bowl and stir to combine.
4. Add the flour mixture to the butter mixture in two or three batches, mixing on low speed just to combine each time. When all the flour has been added and the dough just comes together, turn it onto a lightly floured surface and knead lightly until it's smooth. Don't go overboard with the mixing and kneading; you just want a cohesive mass that's the same color and consistency.
5. For traditional shortbread wedges, divide the dough into two portions and form each into a disc about 3/8 inch (1cm) thick and 7 inches (18cm) in diameter. Put the discs onto the baking sheets and score each one into 8 wedges with a sharp knife. Use a fork to prick holes all over each disc.
6. If you'd like cut-out or stamped cookies, roll portions of dough out between two sheets of parchment paper to your desired thickness. Remove the top sheet of parchment and cut out or stamp cookies. Place on baking sheets, leaving a half inch (1 1/2cm) between each cookie.
7. Bake the shortbread until dry, firm to the touch and just beginning to color at the edges. Discs will take 30-40 minutes and smaller cookies anywhere from 15-25 minutes, depending on their size.
8. Cool the shortbread on the baking sheets for five minutes, then transfer to a cooling rack. When completely cool, store in an airtight container or package up in boxes or bags for gifting.

Best Ever Chocolate Gingerbread Cookies

MAKES
about 48 cookies

PREP TIME
30 min

COOKING TIME
12 min

OVEN SETTINGS
350°F/180°C
Convection
No Steam

INGREDIENTS

1 cup (250g) unsalted butter, cubed, cold from the fridge is fine

1 1/3 cups firmly packed (225g) dark brown sugar

1 cup (325g) golden syrup (I know this can be hard to find in some parts. If you can't get it, substitute with half treacle and half honey. It's different in taste but will similar for color)

6 1/4 cups (775g) all-purpose (plain) flour

1/4 cup (50g) cocoa powder (I use Dutch processed for deeper color and flavor; you can substitute regular unsweetened cocoa)

1 Tbsp plus 1 tsp (18g) baking soda (bicarb soda)

6 Tbsp (30g) ground ginger

1 Tbsp ground cinnamon

1 1/2 tsp ground cloves

1 1/2 tsp ground nutmeg

1/2 tsp ground white pepper

METHOD

1. Preheat your oven to 350°F/180°C, Convection/Fan Forced. Grease or line several cookie sheets and set aside.
2. Put the butter, brown sugar and golden syrup into a medium saucepan and cook over medium heat, stirring, until the butter and sugar have melted and the mixture is smooth. Increase the heat to bring to the boil, then cook for 1 minute before turning off and removing from heat. Allow to cool for 5-10 minutes while you get the rest of the ingredients ready.
3. Sift the flour, cocoa, baking soda and spices into a very large mixing bowl. Give it a whisk to blend the dry ingredients together. In general I can't be bothered sifting ingredients, but here it really is necessary. You don't want lumps of flour or soda in the dough later.
4. Pour the hot mix over the flour mix and use a wooden spoon to stir everything together. It's hard work, but keep mixing until it's smooth with no lumps of flour remaining.

These cookies are a different take on the classic gingerbread recipe you'll find on the Steam & Bake website. They're spicy, sturdy and incredibly popular as a sweet little Christmas gift. I use pre-packaged royal icing mix to pipe pretty designs onto mine, but they're equally lovely with candied fruit or nuts pressed into the top before baking, or simple and unadorned.

If you aren't already in the habit of weighing your ingredients for baking, I strongly suggest you give it a go here. Digital scales are inexpensive and easy to use. I have given cup and spoon measures, but they're open to wild fluctuations in weight, especially with dry ingredients. Different ingredient weights will alter the texture and flexibility of your dough.

This batch size will give you a good four dozen large Christmas shapes, or the panels for a couple of gingerbread houses plus some cookies. Feel free to halve the quantity if that's too much.

The dough is easiest to work with straightaway, when it's warm and pliable. Happily, you can re-knead and re-roll all your scraps as much as you like without really affecting the texture of the finished cookies, so you'll be able to use up every last scrap of dough.

METHOD Continued...

5. Tip the dough onto a clean surface and knead until smooth and firm (if it's too hot, leave the dough for a few minutes until you can handle it). If it's too much to handle as one mass, split it into two or three portions for kneading.
6. Take a portion of your dough and roll it out to 1/4 inch (6mm) thickness. You shouldn't need to flour the surface as this dough is firm and smooth enough to lift cleanly after rolling.
7. Cut your chosen shapes from the rolled dough and lift them gently onto the prepared baking sheets. Leave about half an inch (1.5cm) between each cookie.
8. Bake the cookies until they're just firm to the touch and have lost their sheen. It can be a little hard to tell when these cookies are done because of their deep color, but 12 minutes is my standard time – a little less for thinner or very small cookies, a little more for large gingerbread house panels. Remove from the oven and allow to cool on the baking sheets for a couple of minutes, then transfer to a wire rack to cool completely.
9. Decorate the cookies as you like and store in a well-sealed container, or package into clear bags for gifts.

Burnt Caramel Truffles

MAKES
48 truffles

PREP TIME
45 min

COOKING TIME
40 min

OVEN SETTINGS
115°F/46°C
Steam
100% Humidity

INGREDIENTS

For the burnt caramel
2 cups (400g) granulated sugar
1/2 cup (125ml) water

For the truffles
11 oz (300g) good quality dark/bittersweet chocolate, chopped (I use one with 62% cocoa solids; anything from 55-70% is nice here)
2/3 cup (160ml) heavy whipping cream
1/4 cup (90g) burnt caramel, cooled to room temperature
6 Tbsp (85g) unsalted butter, very soft
About 1 1/2 cups (180g) unsweetened cocoa powder for rolling

METHOD

1. Make the burnt caramel. Put the sugar into a deep saucepan over medium heat and cook, stirring occasionally, until it's melted. Continue to cook until the sugar turns first a golden brown and then black. When it's ready there will be large bubbles breaking on the surface and it will begin to smoke.
2. While the sugar cooks, bring the water to a boil in another saucepan. When the sugar is done, remove it from heat and put a sieve over the pan. Very carefully, wearing an oven mitt to hold the pan of water, pour the boiling water through the sieve into the sugar. It will foam and splutter; the sieve and oven mitt minimize the risk of burns. Once all the water is added and the mixture has settled, give it a stir and then set aside to cool. Store burnt caramel in a lidded jar in the fridge until you need it.
3. Make the truffles. Line an 8 inch (20cm) square cake pan with parchment paper and set aside.

I first used burnt caramel as a flavoring about 15 years ago, after discovering it in the book Chocolate Obsession, by chocolatier Michael Recchiuti. It's hard to describe the exact taste, but think rich, nutty and complex with just a hint of smokiness. It's become a regular addition to my baking and each year you'll find something in my Christmas gift boxes infused with what is essentially blackened sugar. Truffles are a great vehicle for the flavor; they're luxurious and special, and relatively simple to make if you follow the directions methodically.

To make this recipe, you'll first need to make the burnt caramel and let it cool. The truffle mixture also needs to set for several hours, so I prefer to make the caramel and the truffle mixture one day, and roll it into balls the next.

The burnt caramel makes more than you need, but it's difficult to do in a smaller quantity. It keeps indefinitely in the fridge, ready to add a tablespoon or two to your next batch of brownies, cookies or cakes. Try it wherever you'd normally add vanilla.

METHOD Continued...

4. Put the chocolate, cream and burnt caramel (don't forget you've made more caramel than you need for a single batch, so don't use it all!) into a deep glass bowl and cover very well with plastic wrap. You don't want any moisture to be able to get into the bowl. Put the bowl in your steam oven and set to 115°F/46°C, Steam, 100% humidity (if you have a sous vide oven setting, use this instead of steam) Cook until the chocolate is melted through, about 30-40 minutes. Before you take off the plastic wrap, dry the outside of the bowl with a kitchen towel to avoid water getting in. (Note: if your steam oven doesn't operate at such a low temperature, you can do this step using a double boiler over the stove. Be very careful not to overheat the mixture, though. An instant read thermometer is very helpful if you're using this method).
5. Use a balloon whisk to mix the chocolate, cream and burnt caramel together until well combined. It will come together as a glossy mixture, then lose its sheen a little and thicken up. At this point, whisk in the soft butter a tablespoon at a time. The finished product will be quite thick and 'gloopy'.
6. Spread the truffle mixture into the lined pan and let it cool and set at room temperature for 3-4 hours, then wrap well and place in the fridge overnight if you aren't rolling truffles straightaway.
7. Shape and roll the truffles. Turn the slab of truffle mixture onto a clean countertop and cut it into 48 pieces (I cut evenly into 6 strips one way and 8 the other, giving small rectangles). Put the cocoa powder into a wide, shallow bowl.
8. You can simply roll the rectangles in cocoa, or roll each piece into a small ball using cocoa-dusted palms. Roll the balls in cocoa to coat.
9. Store the truffles in a container with extra cocoa so they don't stick together. If you're packaging for gifting, you may want to dust them a second time just before boxing or bagging. These are best kept in the fridge, where they'll last for a week or more. Remove half an hour before serving.

www.ingramcontent.com/pod-product-compliance
Lightning Source LLC
Chambersburg PA
CBHW061807290426
44109CB00031B/2960